The Spi

Peter H. Hackney

2 Co 5:14

The Spirit is Among Us

Renewal and the Local Church

Philip Hacking

Marshall Pickering

Marshall Morgan and Scott
Marshall Pickering
3 Beggarwood Lane, Basingstoke, Hants RG23 7LP, UK

British Library Cataloguing in Publication Data

Hacking, Philip
  The Spirit is Among Us
  1. Fellowship—Religious aspects—
  Christianity
  I. Title
  260   BV4517.5

  ISBN 0-551-01421-0

Text set in Plantin by Brian Robinson, Buckingham
Printed and bound in Great Britain by
Hazell Watson & Viney, Member of the BPCC Group,
Aylesbury, Bucks

Contents

1

Foundations

I am a Christian of the immediate postwar variety, converted at a holiday camp when these were in their blissful infancy. My ordination in Liverpool Cathedral was in 1955 and all seemed relatively calm and optimistic in church life, at least for a young and enthusiatic curate. That curacy was in a working class part of the parish of St Helens, but we were happily free from inner city tensions and the working class was not distant from church life. The challenge was there, but nothing remotely approaching despair.

Thirty years have seen a revolution in society. They have also seen a revolution in church life. So short a time ago the Authorised Version was still the norm and a Church of England service was 1662 verbatim, when to have lay people taking any part in public worship was courageous innovation. The word 'charismatic' was hidden in theological jargon. In a town of evenly matched religious persuasions, Roman Catholics and Protestants were in open conflict. In the evangelical circles you mentioned Keswick in hushed tones, and it held its place unchallenged. Billy Graham had suddenly appeared and at Harringay, as a theological student, my vision was widened and my spiritual pulse quickened.

The student of church history needs a vantage point to assess the balance sheet of gains and losses in the Christian world. But some things are obvious even now. Few would doubt that church worship has gained enormously with its greater flexibility and concern for congregational participation, In theory we all accept the church as the Body of Christ and everymember ministry as the pattern of church life. When I was a student we discussed the place of the laity and now we wonder at the place of the clergy. The wheel has gone full circle. Church unity has become so commonplace, it has almost become tedious. Many churches are oganised to the hilt and move with computerised efficiency.

Yet all is not well. With all the blossoming of life, church attendances barely hold their own. Growing congregations are very often largely at the expense of dying ones. We shuffle the pack rather than make in-roads into secular society. There have been countless grandiose schemes in my thirty years of ministry and some have left very obvious marks. But many have been nine-day wonders and the tide of spiritual renewal has only come in marginally. Folk religion still exists. Christmas is a social phenomenon of intriguing proportions, the last bastion of sentimental religion. Still all but a handful pass from this world with religious words pronounced over them. But I believe the church is now less in touch with the ordinary man and woman, and many contemporary movements in the church make the gap wider. The minister who still visits from door to door is seen as a relic by those trained in all the modern arts of pastoral administration. 'A housegoing parson makes a churchgoing people' was always a somewhat hopeful slogan, but I am still unashamed in my dedication to the principle behind it. In

8

the early years of my ministry I was often rebuked for failure to visit, but now I find frequent expressions of surprise when I appear on the door step.

Perhaps most of all we have lost out on the centrality of biblical and expository ministry. We exalt 'worship' but leave preaching out of that context. There are seminars and courses on drama, dance and the use of audiovisual aids. But with some glorious exceptions, we do not train people to preach, and indeed, we create an atmosphere in which the sermon is seen as almost expendable. In his book *Preaching and Preachers* Dr Martin Lloyd Jones sounds the clarion call: 'Ultimately . . . to me the work of preaching is the highest and the greatest and the most glorious calling to which anyone can ever be called. If you want something in addition to that I would say without any hesitation that the most urgent need in the Christian Church is true preaching; and as it is the greatest and the most urgent need in the Church, it is obviously the greatest need of the world also'. True revival will centre around a rediscovery of the power of the Word and the vitality of a consistent preaching ministry. Otherwise growth will always be exotic and transient, like the shallow soil of our Lord's parable. Spiritual renewal, to which we all pay lip service, is in the New Testament a continuous activity of the Spirit in our lives: 'Though our outer nature is wasting away our inward nature is being renewed every day' (2 Cor. 4:16).

The burden of my ministry increasingly is to encourage this consistency of progress. We are called to be pilgrims, not tourists. Paul speaks of the supreme evidence of the Spirit in the human life in terms of fruit (Gal. 5:22-23). Jesus uses similar analogies in the Upper Room in John chapter 15. Fruit does not appear instantly. There is a natural process even in the supernatural realm. In a world

9

of instant package answers we must beware of being tricked into the expectations of instant holiness.

Similarly we are encouraged to 'be filled with the Holy Spirit' (Eph. 5:18) – yet another reminder of the daily experience. It should not be impossible to create an excitement about normal Christian living. Sadly the best sellers on our over-packed religious bookstalls are the stories which tell the abnormal, true or exaggerated. Balanced Christian living sounds dull by comparison. Therefore we must pack it with New Testament dynamic before too many more casualties appear, products of wild and often unbiblical extremes.

The key lies in the faithful exposition of God's truth. Here the balance will be found, and the bee in the bonnet will be swatted. In this way the amazing promises of Scripture will be set in context, losing some of their apparently attractive extravagance, but offering blessing in greater depth. Here the warnings will be sounded as well. We shall see the miraculous at work and rejoice in it. We shall notice long stretches of revelation with no reference to miracles at all. We shall note the help of the Spirit and find ourselves expecting far more from him. We shall also note the uncomfortable commands of Scripture, demanding daily discipline and obedience, with God expecting far more from us.

It was William Carey, the father of modern missions, who gave us the famous dictum, 'expect great things from God, attempt great things for God'. This is the refreshing balance of Scripture. In the Acts of the Apostles we read of the Spirit leading the church into the divinely given programme of Acts 1:8, 'you shall receive power when the Holy Spirit has come upon you and you shall be my witnesses in Jerusalem, Judea, Samaria and to the ends of the earth'. But he works through the church and through

10

individual Christians, who slowly – often bravely – struggle into obedience. In that human-divine co-operation there were the high days such as the church's birthday at Pentecost, but the everyday experience was equally thrilling: 'The Lord added to the church daily those who were being saved'. This is the blueprint for church growth, and the inspired Scriptures gives us the foundation for that growth in Acts 2:42: 'They devoted themselves to the apostle's teaching and to the fellowship, to the breaking of bread and to prayer'.

The Apostles' teaching speaks of the basic doctrine of the New Testament. Any movement which denies the uniqueness of that revelation has moved into very dangerous waters. The task of every Christian leader is to unravel the mystery of that word and to proclaim boldly its teaching and none other. At my ordination I was given the Bible as the symbol of my authority. To this I am bound. Any fruit in ministry has resulted from that and there are no short cuts. We live in an age when people are wanting a direct word from the Lord without the need to bow before the authority of Scripture. Such subjective Christianity can be disastrous. Mercifully the Lord, by his Spirit, communicates to us today, but every personal revelation must always be subservient to the revealed truth of the New Testament. Publicity stunts, as the church bows to the world's ways, may reap a kind of harvest but it will be transitory and there will be casualties. The history of the church has illustrations galore of this deviation from God's plan. We should build to last and we should bear in mind the final message of Jesus in the sermon on the mount, when he contrasted the house built on the rock and that built on the sand. To build on anything other than the word of God is to build on sand which ultimately will cause collapse.

11

The foundations include 'fellowship', that sharing together which was the great hallmark of the early church and very often utterly practical in its implications. In that early church fellowship clearly different temperaments merged. Even the original apostles, so often divided and weak in the day of Jesus, had found a glorious unity in the Spirit. One of the most vital testimonies to the world is the church at one, with many peripheral differences and yet lovingly united. My experience of God at work over the years of ministry has almost always been based upon a working together of people from different backgrounds but with a united concern for the glory of Jesus. Unity is always one of his great gifts.

That fellowship was seen in the breaking of bread and in prayer, linking with our Lord's ministry in the upper room. The centrality of the Lord's Supper in the early church ensured that the early Christians were united around the cross, glorying not in their Lord's power but in his weakness. We are called not to be ashamed of Christ crucified, but the message of the cross from earliest days was seen by the world as folly and weakness (1 Cor. 1:22-25). Again, we must beware that we do not pander to the world's desire to see signs. Jesus was very unwilling to provide that kind of sign. The sign in which the church will always conquer is the sign of the cross. At that point apparent weakness is turned to strength and folly into divine wisdom.

Prayer was the boomerang which brought the blessing of God down and brought about miracles of every kind. When men and women begin to pray things happen, and the Acts of the Apostles is studded with illustrations of the dynamic of people at prayer. Here is a fundamental of the church which is demanding and therefore not always the priority it ought to be. When Nehemiah, a great man of

God in the Old Testament, began to pray about the needs of his beloved city Jerusalem, very quickly the prayer came back and hit him and caused him to offer his own services. I have never found prayer easy, but I have come to know that without it all else will be in vain.

If we dare to fulfil our part in these priorities we have outlined – Bible teaching, fellowship and prayer – we may expect God to be active afresh in every generation. I have never seen revival and I have rarely been on mountain tops in my spiritual experience, but I have seen the Lord doing his work steadily and consistently and I find every Lord's Day a real foretaste of heaven. Sometimes I have envied Christians who have had such peaks in their Christian lives and yet I have now come to believe that what the Lord has done for me is wonderful beyond explanation. Of course, for all of us there is yet more to come; the best is yet to be. But the glory of the Lord is often seen in the ordinary things, transcending our feeble attempts and our foolish controversies. I have seen lives changed in commonplace ways and find these so often more telling than the more obviously melodramatic sensational stories. We must never despise the day of small things but rejoice to see God at work in the unexpected daily miracles of his grace.

2

A Church Man

When apparently out of the blue the Lord called me to the ministry as a student, there were very differing reactions from friends and family. Although it was totally unexpected to me, others accepted it as almost inevitable: some shook their heads incredulously and others felt that this was a life wasted. Others happily rejoiced and had hope. But the strangest reaction was a phrase I heard quite often: I was accused of 'going into the church'. I wanted to convince my critics that I had been in that church for a very long time. However you define it theologically, I had certainly been in it since conversion and in one sense as a potential member since baptism. Thirty years later, my son also heard that call and yet again the same kind of phrase was heard, not so much from his generation but from mine. It all indicates a very inadequate under- standing of the biblical picture of the church.

In the New Testament the church has a very high profile. It is impossible to be 'in Christ' without being 'in the church'. Evangelical Christians perhaps have too much emphasised the individual response to the gospel and not enough the corporate commitment. One of the best definitions of the church universal and local is found in 1 Corinthians 1:2: 'to the church of God which is at Corinth, to those sanctified in Christ Jesus, called to be saints together with all those who in every place call on the name of Lord Jesus Christ, both their Lord and ours'. Here is the heart of the true unity of the church – 'both their Lord and ours'. All who truly own the Lordship of Christ belong to the family of God. This lies behind the often misunderstood or maligned word 'catholic'. It is quite wrong to allow any one section of the church to claim this as their monopoly. All Christians are part of the catholic church and we should rejoice at that reality. Another word which has almost lost currency is 'ecumenical'. The word means 'of one house' and has dominated modern ecclesiastical thinking and planning. There is a danger that we are so anxious to gather as many as possible into the family that we want to make the house bigger than the New Testament allows it to be. Equally there are Christians whose concept of the faith is so narrow that they can hardly conceive of anyone beyond their own immediate grouping being in that family of God.

One of the joys of my interdenominational background is that long before the word ecumenical became popular, I knew something of the thrill of being in a Christian group where denominations had no significance. I appeared at Keswick for the first time as a student, but I already knew something of the message of its motto, 'All one in Christ Jesus'. I have never found it possible in my ministry to exclude any true believer from the most intimate fellowship of the church where I have ministered. Of course, the table of the Lord should be open to all Christians and I have always disagreed with those who would fence that table from people of other denominational backgrounds. I recollect a phone call when I was a Rector in Edinburgh from the Bishop of that day who had heard that I was allowing members of other churches to take Communion in St Thomas' Church, where I ministered. Apparently someone had complained about this breadth of view (not from St Thomas', I hasten to add) and the Bishop was doing his duty. He inquired what would happen if he ordered me to discontinue that policy. I assured him courteously that I would take no notice. He admitted that he had expected that answer, and diplomatically added that there was nothing more to discuss. I guess that deep down the Bishop was bigger than the so-called rules, and happily the Church of England has now widened those regulations. But I believe that behind this openness at Communion lies the whole concept of the Church of Jesus as the New Testament understands it and as Paul defines it at the beginning of 1 Corinthians, a letter to a church full of dynamic and yet also full of division.

The New Testament obviously has no parallel to our modern denominations, even though each of these tries to find its ancestry there. There is no half-way house between the world-wide church and the local manifestation. Our great reforming fathers understood this very well and in the Articles of Religion in the 1662 prayer book Anglicans are reminded that 'the visible church of Christ is a congregation of faithful men in which the pure Word of God is preached and the sacraments be duly ministered'. People, not buildings, make the church and the activity carried on by these people is the mark of a real church family. The church is not created by its organisation but by the divine activity happening within it.

It is impossible to turn the clock back, and denominational structures have inevitably been produced. It may well be argued that different temperaments will always respond in different ways of worship and structures of church government. There could be a variety which lends richness to the church of Jesus Christ. Also there is a real sense in which a national church has its own particular value. I still appreciate the privilege of being able to knock on doors as the minister of the parish in which the people live, and by and large this is respected. There are many attendant dangers of nominalism for people who like to have some vague allegiance to the local parish church. But the situation also presents endless opportunities. I have been increasingly convinced that the greatest evangelistic opportunity within our country at this point in time is the funeral service. It seems a strange fact that on such an occasion most people are found in a church building. The sensitivity required is very obvious, but the challenge is there. We cannot miss this particular opening for the good news of Jesus to people at a time of loss and personal sense of need.

But in 1 Corinthians Paul has no thought of a national church or denominations. He is very concerned to demonstrate the sinfulness of division within the church of Jesus Christ. In this first chapter of 1 Corinthians he has strong words to say about those who divide up the family of God (1 Cor. 1:10-14).

Denomination may be a comparatively modern phenomenon, but the party spirit or sectarianism has always been around. It was there in Corinth in abundance and Paul is adamant that Christians who gather round personalities or ideas are in danger of denying the truth of the gospel. He denounces the personality cult that was rampant, including those who claimed allegiance to Paul himself. In the midst of his condemnation he also attacks the group who say, 'I belong to Christ' (1 Cor. 1:12). Almost certainly that speaks of the pure church mentality,

17

the group which arrogantly claimed to be above all parties and professed to be the true church of Jesus Christ.

How terribly contemporary it all is. Personalities often unconsciously gather people around themselves, as Paul discovered. In small ways ministers in churches have to suffer from this disease. Sometimes it is the reverse side of a very lovely loyalty. But how tragic when personality figures obscure Jesus Christ! Each one of us who has a position of leadership in the church needs constantly to be ready to hide behind the cross. The more prominent the ministry the more dangerous the problem becomes. There is an awesome temptation for those who stand on platforms or those who speak with power from pulpits. How much they need the prayers of God's people. Sadly there are others, like the false prophets throughout Scripture, who love the plaudits of men and, like the Pharisees, delight in positions and titles (Mt. 23:5-12).

Into this distasteful picture comes the group which would claim to be above everything which spoils the church, and here is often the greatest danger. We have seen in our present age a disenchantment with much about denominationalism, and this can be a very healthy thing. Sometimes we see the rise of leaders who deny the truth of God; sometimes it is the deadness of churches which have lost their vision. We live also in an age when it is comparatively easy for men and women with strident voices to dominate the media and draw attention to themselves. We are therefore the more ready to hear the siren voices drawing us to their particular church, which they claim to be completely pure. We are often being exhorted to leave the sinking ship of denominationalism and to join that perfect church, which is absolutely true to Scripture. I believe the apostle Paul would exhort us to beware. There is no perfect church this side of heaven.

18

Our loyalty is to our Lord himself, in whom is perfection. Then we are called to a spirit of faithfulness and not un-questioning obedience to the local church into which God has called us. Unless that church turns away signally from the truth or denies the very essence of the gospel, there we should stay and bear our witness faithfully. The church always stands under the cross, proud of that message which has brought it life and at the foot of the cross we all stand equal, whatever our affiliation or our religious label.

It is a healthy corrective always to recollect that my church is in fact not my church but 'the church of God'. It is the creation of the Holy Spirit, who always brings order out of chaos and creates the kind of dynamic unity which is the pattern of the New Testament and so different from the dull uniformity of man-made schemes of church order. The church is our Lord's by redemption and because of the Lordship of Jesus, who is the head of the church. The word for church means 'a called-out people', with a reminder that the church is meant to be like her Lord – in the world yet separate from it. Only in that way can we function as salt and light. The apostle John has a wonderful way of drawing attention to this by two very parallel verses. In his gospel in Chapter 1:18 he says, 'No one has ever seen God; only the Son, who is in the bosom of the Father, he has made him known' and in his first epistle Chapter 4:12 he writes, 'No man has ever seen God; if we love one another, God abides in us and his love is perfected in us'. To add these two together brings the uncomfortable challenge that just as Jesus reflects God to the world, so the church must reflect Jesus to the world. We are called to be those who actually make Jesus real, not just in our own individual lives but within our fellowship together. The old church fathers had a phrase which went, 'ubi christus ibi ecclesia'. That defines the church perfectly: 'where Christ is, there is the church'.

In this context, we should look at the lovely analogies of the church, particularly found in Paul's letter to the Ephesians. We are called to be the building of which he is the foundation stone, the body of which he is the head and the bride of whom he is the bridegroom (Eph. 2:19-22; 4:15-16; 5:25-27). That same letter insists that the church is seen in the world as the fulness of Christ (1:23). You could not have a higher picture of the church. There was a time when evangelicals were known as 'low churchmen'. I have always fought against that connotation and believe that in the truer sense of the word I am a 'high churchman' because I must take that church seriously. It is the church of God. I would testify that I have seen so much of the richness of Jesus because I have been privileged to share in many expressions of that body of Christ throughout the world. Yet I would also bear testimony that it is in the local church where I am most known and where I can be most hurt that I experience that richness at the deepest level. It is comparatively easy to enjoy fellowship in a fortnight's ministry in some overseas church. It is another thing to be real in the rough and tumble of life, where the warts are very evident on our own faces and the faces of our fellow Christians. Yet there love can dominate and the church of God can be the greatest audio-visual presentation of all time.

But Paul writes not to the vague church of God; rather to the church of God 'which is at Corinth'. Always the local church will be affected by the culture of the world in which it lives. We must relate to that world and we must translate our gospel in terms that can be understood in that world. Indeed we must clothe the gospel with flesh in our contemporary society. But we must beware of allowing the ideas of the world to seep into the church. Jesus related to people of his age and he was a friend of publicans and

20

sinners, but in no way did he allow himself to be moulded by the world's ideas of his day.

The church at Corinth has a close relationship with the church in 'every place'. It is tragic when we try to ape the churches of other places. I can recollect preaching in a cathedral in India and being distressed to see that everything followed the pattern of an Anglican cathedral in England, seemingly quite out of touch with the culture surrounding it. I can accept the value of some consistent pattern of worship. In its day that was the glory of the Church of England or the Church of Rome. But I would expect that churches in different places would reflect in the patterns of worship and the style of church government the surrounding contemporary culture. The message must not be changed, but the outward trappings which mean so much to so many should vary. I believe we have never really faced the challenge of making worship in the inner city areas relevant, and we have constantly been guilty of assuming that the culture in which we grew up as Christians must be the only kind of Christian culture. I can recollect my first visit to the Netherlands, when I was offered by a good evangelical pastor a glass of whisky and a cigar. I hastily declined the offer, trying not to feel indignant as a traditional English evangelical. However, I learned in conversation afterwards that my host was clearly horrified at the fact that I watched television! In the externals we had differing views of what suited an evangelical Christian, but we discovered that in depth we had the same message, the same faith and the same Lord. The uniting factor within the church of God wherever it may happen to be is our allegiance to the name of our Lord Jesus Christ. Christians are seen as those who call upon his name in worship and obedience.

St Paul has an obsession with the name of Jesus. Nine

times in the first nine verses of 1 Corinthians he gives him his title. He is marvellously Christ-centred, and so must we be within the life of the Church. The name 'Christian' is a glorious name, transcending all else. It is sad that we find ourselves having to qualify the name Christian because it has so often been debased. We have to talk about 'born again Christians' or 'evangelical Christians'. May the true meaning of the name become resurrected, and may we simply be proud to be those who name the name of Jesus.

If we take the name of Jesus and our relationship within the Church seriously then we shall go that stage further and be a group of people who are determined on a life of holiness. We are called to be saints and we are being sanctified (1 Cor. 1:2). Holiness should always be the hallmark of the people of God, and holinesss is likeness to Christ.

Corinth was infamous for its evil practices. 'To play the Corinthian' was a synonym for gross sexual immorality. There was therefore a very clear mark of distinction between the Christian community and the local moral standards. That comes out frequently in Paul's letter, not least in chapter 6:9-11, where he reminds the Christians what they once were, and that now things were different.

In our society today we are moving in that direction. The general acceptance of the Christian ethic in Britain has been lost and wide moral divergencies have appeared. A whole generation thought that it could keep the Christian ethic while throwing overboard the Christian doctrine. It has been tragically demonstrated that this does not work. It may be seen in all kinds of ways, not least in the realm of sexual morality. Any local minister is very aware of the challenge he faces in the preparation of couples for marriage. We have taken this so seriously in our own church that we have recently instituted a course of preparation (which has been generally well received) in order to highlight the meaning of Christian marriage, so rarely understood by many of those who get married in church. All too often the minister is conscious that the couples he prepares for marriage have indulged in pre-marital sexual intercourse and many of them are living together already.

There is also the moral chaos over the homosexual issue, where any Christian who dares to condemn homosexual practice is seen as unloving. It is impossible to hold on to the authority of Scripture and to accept the validity of a homosexual relationship (cf Rom. 1:24-27). In this age of moral indifference where tolerance is the highest virtue, to stand by Christian ethics is to be marked out as very different. This is the challenge of holiness, which means to be set apart.

Inevitably there are many grey areas in the ethics of daily living. I happen to be a minister of a church which contains a very high percentage of professional people in business, medicine, education and industry. In all these realms the problem of following the way of Christ is not simple. The challenge to the preacher is to expound those principles to guide the church member in the decisions which he or she has to make day by day. We are wise not to be dogmatic where Scripture does not allow us to be so. But it is in the daily living where the reality of a conversion to Christ is often most obviously seen. New life will always involve new lifestyle. We are called to follow the example of Jesus by living within the world as part of it, yet being set apart in our ways.

There is always a danger of extremes. On the one extreme are those who hive off in some kind of monastic way of living, in a total Christian community set apart from the normal everyday existence of the secular world around us. Jesus never asked us to leave the world in that particular manner, although for a tiny minority it may be right for a particular purpose or a specified time. On the other extreme there is the danger of being so absorbed in the world in which we live that we cease to have any witness. We find ourselves being conditioned by the standards and ways of society. The Christian ethic must always be related to our world; it must never be conditioned by it. Biblical holiness never changes, although its manifestation must be seen in contemporary garb.

If the emphasis on Christian witness must be in terms of holiness of life rather than excitement of worship, the two do not necesssarily conflict. In 1 Corinthians 1:2 the church is defined as the fellowship of those who 'call on the name of our Lord Jesus Christ, both their Lord and ours'. Calling on the name of our Lord is a shorthand for the act of worship and was first found in Genesis 4:26 when 'men began to call upon the name of the Lord'. Worship means in the first place an acknowledgement of the lordship of God, and in the Christian context, the lordship of Jesus. It is staggering that the Old Testament verses which speak of God's lordship are often used in the New Testament to speak of Jesus and his authority. But worship must go with life, and we are urged constantly in the Bible not just to call him Lord but to obey him as Lord. There can be no mature worship without constant reference to Scripture in which we find the truth about the Lord whom we are called to worship.

It is not surprising that the word 'Christian' was coined in the days of the early church for those who spoke so often about Christ or Messiah. The name first appears in Acts 11:25 in the city of Antioch, and the story of that city

24

is a perfect illustration of the kind of church the Lord means us to be. Antioch is seen as a church which was truly alive, brought into being by a bold proclamation of the Lord Jesus to Jews and Greeks alike and often by quite anonymous Christian people.

It was also a church which learned, and we read in Acts chapter 11 of a whole year's ministry of teaching by Saul and Barnabas. No church will prosper unless it is consistently growing in knowledge.

Then it became a church which loved, responding to a challenge to give to Christians in need – the first 'Christian Aid' venture of history. Not surprisingly it then became the first overseas missionary sending church in Acts chapter 13, sending out its leaders into the pioneer missionary work of that day.

Not every local church has these marks in the manner of Antioch. But I deem it a privilege that it was in a local church that I was reborn, and from that local church I was sent out in service, and my ministry has been in that kind of local church ever since. Movements which submerge the local church need to be watched carefully. All great movements should serve the local church. I have been privileged to work recently alongside Billy Graham, and I believe one of the hallmarks of his greatness in the Lord's service is that he is so dedicated to serving the local church. In that church we live and grow and serve.

3

A Parish Man

My spiritual pilgrimage is largely the tale of four churches, supplemented by forays into churches of all denominations and in every part of the country. Not many Anglicans will have been privileged to address would-be ministers of the Free Church of Scotland or to preach in ecumenical services within the Roman Catholic communion. I have a principle of being happy to preach anywhere where the full liberty of preaching the gospel is allowed. I have also led over thirty parish missions in many parts of England, mostly in the north, and in Northern Ireland. This local evangelism is the perfect setting, because follow-up is already tailor-made. It may not produce the most spectacular results, but I have been encouraged down the years to see the lasting fruits of this kind of parish evangelism. Inevitably the patterns have changed and often in these days the focal point is the home group, the men's breakfast, the ladies' luncheon club and fewer straight preachments in the local church. But people are more naturally drawn into these groups to hear the gospel and can more effectively be cared for pastorally after the week of evangelism is past.

Any local church must present its imperfections as well

as its joys to the world. I have often been tempted to write the stories of the churches in which I have been privileged to live and serve. But I fear that the 'warts and all' picture might not always be appreciated by parishioners past and present. The itinerant preacher largely avoids the pains and the joys of pastoral care, while the local minister is utterly immersed in the lives of his flock. There is no substitute for the intimacy of this ministry, but it can be costly indeed. Over the years I have discovered the depth of the meaning in Paul's pastoral phrases in his letters when he speaks of 'the care of all the churches'; where he talks of pangs of childbirth until he sees Christ being formed in his believers; where he can talk about being a father to the folk or a nursemaid. The analogies rush through his pages and the picture is of a man who did not preach from a distance nor prayed by rote but was agonisingly linked in the most personal way with the people in the churches he pioneered or served.

My pilgrimage began in a fairly new local parish church in Blackburn in Lancashire. There I first cast anchorage in my spiritual life. There I was born and bred until University days. All else began there: meeting my wife, getting addicted to the joys of cricket and football and being well grounded in a solid educational system. But most important, there I found Christ and found him within the context of the local church, for which I have always been grateful.

The Church of the Saviour is a solidly evangelical church and in my younger days had a good Protestant element within it. Prayer and Bible study and expository teaching were the order of the day, and I discovered the joy of seeing the treasures of the Bible being unfolded. It was a church where young people liked to gather and I was attracted to Christ not least because of the qualities of

27

young people slightly older than myself. In the true sense of the word it was a family church, not a child-centred one. Many of my convictions and many of my hang-ups were born here.

Against all usual expectations, in this a predominantly working-class parish there was great spiritual life. From my own road of terraced houses four of us were ordained within a matter of a few years. Somehow it does not quite fit the normal, rather pessimistic view of the church's ministry among the working-class. I was the twenty-first from my church to be ordained in a very short period of time.

All this demonstrates the work of the Spirit in a local church. We did not talk too much about the Spirit in those immediate post war days, and we missed much. But there was no doubt that the Spirit was at work, and I fear that sometimes an undue emphasis upon the Spirit actually restricts him rather than allows him to work. We made much of Jesus, and that is surely the Spirit's work.

There was an intimacy in those pre-war, wartime and post-war years that has probably gone forever. There was a sense of community, both for the good and the bad. Each one knew his neighbour and sometimes that knowledge expressed itself in gossip rather than care. But certainly people belonged to each other.

As a child I learned to appreciate the importance of the study of the word of God. Scripture Union notes were in my young hands, and I have often marvelled that the day would come when I would actually be writing some of those notes! As teenagers we were encouraged even in those days to lead our own youth groups and to be involved in Christian witness. Before the guitar was sanctified, we had a singing group which went around the neighbourhood, musically very ordinary but spiritually very significant – at least for the singers! Worship was strictly by the Prayer Book, but not without life and vigour, and we must have been one of the first churches to start regular guest services. I learned evangelism early in life. My commitment to Jesus was in one sense a natural growth into the truth, but there was a point of open commitment at a holiday camp when I stood up and gave my life to the Lord. Nowhere but the local church can be the seedbed of that kind of growth and commitment.

At the age of nineteen for the first time in my life I moved away from home to read history at Oxford. It was a traumatic change of environment for someone very conscious of coming from the north and very much in awe of my public school contemporaries – until I discovered that on the cricket field I could be well their equal and, in spite of their apparent erudition, even in the classroom I was not noticeably left behind. My faith was challenged intellectually for the first time, and that was an experience of great significance.

At Oxford I was called to the ministry in a dramatic way. The Lord made me forcibly aware of his call, because I was so slow to hear him speaking. That taught me the lesson that often the spectacular stories of calling are for those who fail to respond to the more normal promptings of the Spirit. But I am glad that I did have that dramatic experience to give me some sensitivity to those in whom the Spirit works in unusual ways.

I owe much to the fellowship of the Christian Union at Oxford, to the guidance of my contemporaries and particularly to an older group of men still left over from the war days. Their maturity strengthened me considerably. But my call to the ministry was more in the context of the church I knew in Lancashire than within the context of a Christian Union, which must always be the handmaid to the church and not more.

In the early days of my training for the ministry so many of my contemporaries had very little knowledge of parish life. They had come to Christ through different kinds of para-church activities: Crusaders, camps, Christian Unions. From that kind of background, with its sometimes intense form of Christianity, it was very difficult for them to relate to the steady, often slow workings of a local church. Mercifully the Lord had led me in a different way, and so I was prepared when my call to the ministry landed me in another working-class situation in St. Helens, Lancashire.

Then I turned my collar round. In the days of the compulsory clerical collar of the good solid variety this was quite an event. To walk down the streets of St Helens was an ordeal at first, assuming that everyone could tell that this new shiny collar spoke of one newly ordained. No doubt I had over-optimistic views of the interest in clergymen and I felt I had to speak to everyone just in case there lurked an anonymous church member ready to complain about the unfriendliness of the new curate. My training had been at Oak Hill College in North London, a good evangelical foundation still fairly young in those days. The staff was small, but I learned so much from the down-to-earth, homely pastoral experience of the Principal, Leslie Wilkinson, and the deep biblical exegesis of Alan Stibbs, who taught many of us to love the Word and to stand by it at all costs. I fear that not always have theological colleges followed that kind of tradition. The blend of parish experience and loyalty to Scripture nurtured many of us in those formative years.

Ordination day in Liverpool Cathedral was moving, even though I have never been a person for ritual. I tend to smile at pomp and ceremony and feel a little awkward within it. Afterwards I was dropped from the coach taking my supporters home to Blackburn, and I was now ordained in a parish which had boasted many curates in the past and was the home of rugby league and Beechams pills. It also had a large parish church, where I was to learn the trade under a gracious Vicar, Bill Bailey.

Practical theology comes as much from experience as from study, and the two must always blend. I am grateful that I started my ministry in very much a parish church which took seriously the responsibilities of caring for the thousands of people living within its boundaries. St. Helens parish was a mixture, but the part of the parish which became my own baby was decidedly a working-class community. I had to learn quickly to smile at history. St. Helens had bred famous curates in its time, including one who became Bishop Chavasse and is still no doubt remembered as the curate who played regularly for the Rugby League team and made his name in that unique way. We were often reminded of the old days when the vast parish church was supposed to be filled on every occasion. It was humbling to realise how insignificant the new young curate was. I entered this parish on the back of Billy Graham, little realising how much I was going to owe to him in days to come. Relays from one of his large crusades had been held in the parish church and for once the 1500 seater building had been filled to capacity. There was still an atmosphere of expectancy and I thank God for it.

The parish church with its largeness was exciting. It was also very demanding in the pre-amplification days when clergy had to learn to throw their voices. Soon I was in charge of my mission church in the working-class area and we saw that steady growth which I see as the norm for effective evangelism. There was door-to-door visitation and every Monday staff meeting we had to give an account of how many doors had been opened to us. It could all be a little artificial and there were ways and means of boosting numbers at the last minute! But I am so glad that I learned that discipline.

It was a parish with strong church links and I found a certain pride in belonging to the parish church. As a good evangelical Christian I had early been enthusiastic about an individual's relationship to the Lord. Now I knew how important the church was in the economy of God. Not least I saw men coming to faith, and the men's meetings which began in my day became so large that they had to break into different groups. After those days, I can never believe that working-class men will not listen to the gospel. For the first time I was able to expound Scripture consistently in a pulpit which had become my own, and that school room which on a Sunday became a church became the very gate of heaven to a number of people.

Ambitiously I started guest services, and slowly people began to respond. There was nothing spectacular, but I knew there was no short cut to encouraging people into church and to faith. Perhaps most of all I appreciated the value of the contacts made on special occasions such as baptisms, weddings and funerals. Of the latter there seemed to be no end, and perhaps my increasing belief that here is the greatest evangelistic opportunity of most churches stems from that day.

It was a hard three years of constant slog, and I marvel now how my wife and young baby survived the lack of attention from husband and father. But I still believe that only in that way are souls really won. Hard work alone brings nobody to Christ, but without hard work very few are won.

My testimony to God's providence is that I rarely see it while it is happening but look back with constant amazement at the way in which God's pattern works out in experience. Such was my call out of the blue to ministry in Scotland at the beginning of 1959. Until I went to check over the church of St. Thomas in Edinburgh I had never been North of the Border, nor had my wife. We had no qualifications whatsoever for ministering to a joint Anglo-Scottish community. But the Lord had his plans.

It was somewhat awe-inspiring to discover that I was the youngest Rector in Scotland at the time, and God had called me to a church where much had happened in the past but congregations were low and spirits probably even lower. Yet there remained a faithful remnant hoping for God to move.

In the providence of the Lord I experienced this ten-year ministry as an 'Anglican Non-conformist'. Scotland grew to be by no means a foreign land but a land of great joy and promise. I even got to the stage when, travelling across the border and seeing the phrase, 'haste ye back to Scotland', I felt a tug at the heart strings. A mere Sassenach, I was amazingly once asked to give a speech at a Bobby Burns banquet. Wisely I refused to put that graciousness to the test!

I see the plan now. The Lord wanted me to see what it was like not to depend upon the normal machinery of a Church of England parish, nor to have the props of a good team of other clergymen around me. There was a certain loneliness in the situation and yet I learned through that the joy of working with eager laity and also the sheer excitement of daring to step out alone. In a strange way I discovered things about the Church of England which I positively enjoyed while at the same time having more and more fellowship with people of other denominations.

In that context we saw the Lord at work steadily but

surely. We tried to organise our church on a pseudo-parish basis, discovering in the process how people hid behind a Presbyterian name when obviously church-going was a thing of the past for them.

The student ministry began there in Edinburgh, and over the years it has been a very firm part of the ministry the Lord has given to me. Even though the church was busy, there was still less administration than in a parish in England and so I was free to travel as an itinerant speaker. Here again I discovered how the Lord was opening doors which he wanted me to enter. How wise it is to let him provide the agenda in his own time and in his own way.

In 1963 I made my first visit to Keswick, and it was a lovely touch of the Lord that my dear mother, who had faithfully prayed for me, learned that I was to speak at Keswick just before she died in that year. It was a somewhat awesome experience to stand alongside men who were great names and whom I had never been privileged to meet. Little did I know then that I was being prepared for further responsibilities in the future.

In Edinburgh too I was learning the challenge of city evangelism, chairing a committee which launched a great crusade in the city with Stephen Olford in the Usher Hall. It may seem a far cry from the enormous administration of Mission England and a Billy Graham Grusade, but for a young man it was very testing yet very rewarding.

I was also learnng that evangelism would divide churches. To my sadness I discovered some evangelical communities who seemed lacking in enthusiasm to join in united ventures, perhaps hiding behind theology or genuinely not able to see that this was one way in which the Lord would work. It always struck me that mass evangelism was on the church's agenda right from the beginning and the Day of Pentecost. Was there ever a greater mass evangelistic day than that? Naturally I discovered ministers with a fear of evangelism but at the same time I found that there was no better uniting force than being engaged in seeking to win people to the Lord.

My ministry was being broadened in so many ways and yet always based on the solid foundation of that local church's ministry. The development has continued and I have always found that even when ministering elsewhere alone I have felt part of my family church. Even before I discovered in depth the pattern in the Acts of the Apostles I had worked out in experience that it is not enough to go alone in Christian service, but always to go as part of a living church family.

Alongside that discovery I was also seeing enacted before my very eyes the parable of the mustard seed. There were high points in our church's growth but very few spectacular moments. What counted was the steady work of consistent preaching, systematic visitation, encouraging lay people in caring and a watchful eye on a balanced worship. All these were the mix that went into a growing church. Such is the pace of life today that if I were to go back into the worship and life of St Thomas I would find a very marked difference. The church in Edinburgh has moved on and I have moved on. But at the time we were moving in step with the Spirit. That is a lesson I am always learning. Rushing on ahead produces problems, and through fear or faithlessness dragging behind will always quench his work. It is always worthwhile trying to keep in step with him.

Our call to Sheffield in the autumn of 1968 on the whole brought a shower of commiserations from our Scottish friends. Sheffield is a much maligned city and we were soon to discover its delights, in a parish not too far from the glories of the Peak District. It also brought an unexpected bonus in that soon I was an ardent supporter of Sheffield Wednesday, and this has become one of the abiding passions of my life outside the work of God's kingdom. All Christian workers need to have some insignificant cause into which they can inject their pent-up frustrations. The Kop at Hillsborough has been a blessed place of refuge now for many years!

I very quickly recognised the joys and demands of parish work in Sheffield. In Scotland I had been released from many of the chores of a vicar in the Church of England. But equally quickly I discovered the opportunities of being a local minister in a church where people come wanting babies baptised, hoping to be married, needing the church's service in times of bereavement. For eighteen years I have been privileged to see the Lord at work. It is not a spectacular story but it is a very significant one. I believe that the Lord has taught me and through me many other people a lesson that his work is often done patiently, consistently and gradually. It is not unimportant that in Scripture the most common word for the Christian life is 'the walk', and walking is a steady exercise.

I have seen too many disasters to be foolish enough to comment on a work in which I am still engaged. Standing close to the canvas, you may not see the total picture. I shall leave others to evaluate what has happened in Christ Church Fulwood during these years. But of some things there can be no doubt. It has been an exciting story of growing congregations, of extending the church building and of providing extra facilities in the shape of hall, lounge and youth centre. There has been a corresponding breakthrough into the community and, although there is a significant eclectic ministry, particularly amongst students, the major work has been done in the neighbour-hood, witnessing for Christ.

The parish of Fulwood is largely a home for young professional people and that has its particular challenge to make the gospel relevant. Indeed, in a recent survey it was discovered that this particular parliamentary constituency has in fact the highest percentage of graduates of any constituency in Britain. In some ways that calls for a ministry that challenges the mind without forgetting that the gospel must be for the whole man and that not all the parish of Fulwood are intellectual giants! The student ministry which goes alongside the local ministry is not in any way a distraction, and there is a wealth of leadership within the church which has given us the opportunity to launch out into new patterns of ministry without being rashly innovative.

The concept of pastoral leadership has grown over the past few years. A vicar who was taught to lead from the front does not always find it easy to share leadership, and I had my own problems of adjustment. But there has been a growing together and now the pastoral work is shared by a number of people who look after part of the parish and take on the pastoral care of their neighbourhood. Each of our home groups comes within the orbit of one of these pastoral leaders and in that way the church has a structure which is suited to growth and individual care and helps to make a large congregation somewhat more of an intimate fellowship or series of fellowships.

Such a structure does allow me the privilege of being free for other kinds of ministry, and I have found it increasingly important that these are all based within the fellowship of the local church. Here I find the ability through the church's prayer and resources to go out in evangelism and preaching ministry in different parts of the country and overseas. The church itself is enriched when it begins to widen its horizons. There is always a two-way process involved and I believe many churches are impoverished because they become much too parochial and inward-looking. The devil always delights to encourage Christians to keep examining themselves and forgetting that there is a world to be won. My experience is that growth in holiness tends to go alongside a real concern to reach others. Nothing is more challenging to my own life than to be used in the preaching of the gospel.

A growing church can become a self-sufficient church, especially when it has rich leadership. As yet we have not found all the answers, but one of the answers we have discovered is to be involved as a church unit in evangelism throughout the city and in other parts of the country. Wherever possible I take with me people from the church bearing witness to their faith and using their particular gifts in music or drama. In this way two objectives are achieved. It makes the evangelistic thrust personal and it means that even as I am reaching out in other parishes I am still acting as vicar of my own church and encouraging my folk in their own spiritual maturity. Sometimes this has been through our complete involvement in major evangelistic enterprises in the city. Twice I have chaired crusades led by my good friend the late David Watson and more recently in the massive Mission England-Sheffield conducted by Billy Graham.

These extra evangelistic thrusts strengthen the local church both by adding to it and by giving its members a focal point for Christian witness and service.

In other ways my years at Sheffield have broadened my own horizons, with several opportunities of ministry abroad, particularly through the SUM Fellowship, an interdenominational missionary society working largely now in North Nigeria, of which for ten years I was chairman. This necessitated visits to Nigeria, and I believe that in all this broadening of my own vision of the world church the local church has benefited and received its own vision. In so doing I think I have been discovering the lesson learned so quickly in the early church that all missionary service is rooted in a particular church family. It was in this spirit that the church at Antioch sent out Barnabas and Saul for the first overseas missionary venture, and when they returned it was to the local church they brought their testimony of what the Lord had done. Without this strong foundation there is a missing dimension. The secret of missionary activity still lies within the local Christian family. How glad I am that I have been privileged to serve in such a local church in various places.

Thought through, it becomes obvious that the health of the church of Jesus in the world is highly dependent upon the vitality of that local manifestation of the body of Christ, so often sadly neglected.

4

The Church – A Theatre

⚜

The church is meant to be a great theatre. Drama has come back into the life of the church, and that is generally accepted as a step forward – or rather backward, because drama and the church have had happy links in the past. But the whole life of the church should be in the truer sense theatre, the demonstration of the reality of God's grace. There is no visual aid like the life of the church.

For better or for worse our life together preaches a message. Throughout Scripture God's purpose in calling out a community is primarily to show clearly his love and grace. In the Old Testament this was the purpose of the call of Israel. Moses had to remind his people that they were not chosen because of their particular gifts or greatness but rather the reverse. As a small and insignificant nation, their only greatness was as a demonstration of what God could do with the apparently unimportant. Hilaire Belloc coined the famous little rhyme, 'How odd of God to choose the Jews'. I take it that this was no racist comment but a truly biblical one. The real Jew thanked God not that he was better than others but that his God was greater than all other gods. But with that great privilege went the solemn responsibility that the

Jewish people should so live that the name of God would be honoured and not blasphemed. From time to time the prophets spoke very sternly about the way in which God's name was dragged in the dirt because of the way of life of the people who owned his name.

Such a concept spills over into the New Testament. Peter sees the church as the new Israel and reminds them in great Old Testament tones that 'you are a chosen race, a royal priesthood, a holy nation, God's own people, that you may declare the wonderful deeds of Him who called you out of darkness into his marvellous light' (1 Pet. 2:9). Paul himself has a similar, revolutionary thought in Ephesians 3:10 where he speaks of the plan that 'through the church the manifold wisdom of God might now be made known'. The church is to be a display of God's grace and power. Later in the same chapter he speaks of 'glory in the church and in Christ Jesus' (3:21). Primarily this message reminds us that the church will show in its very being God as a God of Grace, accepting sinners and changing them. The church will also show the ability of God to break down man-made barriers and create a new community in Christ Jesus. It will also speak of a revelation of God's power by doing those things that cannot be explained without reference to God. We must beware of a foolish seeking after signs and wonders, but we must certainly not run in the opposite direction and expect nothing supernatural to happen. We were amused in our church to discover that we were insured against 'an act of God'. No doubt that is a very good insurance policy phrase, but it is incongruous in church life. Sadly most churches might well go through their existence without ever having claim on such an insurance policy! May there be constant acts of God. All these are the ways in which the church is a visual aid of what God is doing and what God is like.

Such a vision will save Christians from a selfish concept of their own calling and spirituality. Because we live in a self-centred and man-centred world we too often think in terms of our own feelings, our own progress and our own well being. The New Testament is a different world altogether. Jesus promises the power of the Spirit in Acts 1:8 so that the disciples might become witnesses throughout the world. Paul speaks of gifts of the Spirit being given 'for the common good' (1 Cor. 12:7). That is the thrust of New Testament thinking. Whatever God has done for us is meant to be exhibited to others so that the glory might come to God. So Paul could rejoice that when he who had been a persecutor of the church became a preacher of the gospel, all people would marvel and would bring praise to God: 'and they glorified God because of me' (Gal. 1:24). William Temple is said to have commented that the church is unique in being organised for the sake of the people who do not belong. The church is not a club for like-minded people; it is not even just a fellowship of spiritually-minded people. It is a signpost to God for the world.

This principle should affect all our church planning. In our worship we must never degenerate to the level of merely seeking to do things we enjoy. All should be for the glory of God and the best we can offer to him. But we should also always have in mind the outsider who may stumble into our worship or be invited as a guest. Paul has a concern for this when he is writing to the Corinthians and insists that such an outsider should not be able to go away thinking that Christians are mad, but rather should have to bow in acknowledgement that God is in the midst of the congregation and in control (1 Cor. 14:23-25). It was said of the early church that it had this remarkable balance of being somewhat fearsome to outsiders because of the judgments that happened within it and yet at the same time attractive, so that many people were drawn into its fellowship. No church should make it easy for people to belong by lowering standards. But every church should make it easy for people to feel that they want to belong. Our services ought to have a quality of the supernatural about them so that men and women are brought humbly before God. There also must be a note of normality so that a non-Christian might recognise that these are people of their world, but with an answer that they have not yet found.

As in worship, so in fellowship we must be mindful of the people we are seeking to draw into the fellowship. Nothing is more calculated to kill any fellowship group than its inability to reach out to new people. A group which remains static year after year is inevitably going into spiritual bankruptcy. In our planning for all our fellowship groups we must bear in mind the effect they will have on the one who comes new and not conditioned by our ways and our jargon. There must be an openness about our groups, but not the threatening kind that makes the outsider shudder. There must be a love and welcome, but not the over-exuberant, smothering kind that makes the timid newcomer want to escape immediately. In our discussion we must ever be mindful that there are those who know little of the gospel. That does not mean that we need to adopt an undue simplicity and certainly not a patronising attitude to the one who is seeking, but it does mean that we shall be anxious not to give the impression of spiritual one-up-manship in our conversation and attitude.

In the New Testament we have the vision of heaven as the place where the divine plan for the church will ultimately be fulfilled Then the bride of Christ will be perfectly ready for the wedding day and the whole community of God's people will proclaim by their very being the greatness of the triumph of God's grace. All types and nations will be gathered together into one and all the barriers will be down. This will never happen fully this side of heaven. But we are urged in Scripture to be preparing for that day, and we do pray for God's will to be done on earth as in heaven. Perhaps the two greatest ingredients that go into the preparation for that day are holiness and worship. Christians being dedicated to both these great goals will condition all that happens in the life of the church. Since heaven will be entirely dedicated to the glory of God, we should prayerfully aim for that end within the life of the local church. How easily we degenerate into seeking the glory of our own particular church, our own pet theory or way of going about things! It is a mark of mature Christianity that we are only concerned that God be glorified in all that we do and are.

'See how these Christians love one another!' is a comment from early church days. Sadly, it has often been quoted with sarcasm in more recent years, when originally it was said in utter sincerity. The most telling witness of the church is that it focuses the love of God in a way which can be seen and understood by people in the neighbourhood. The world does not expect perfection of any Christian group but it has a right to expect sincerity and integrity. There will be a readiness to accept the fallen Christian with the proviso that such a Christian does not seek to explain away his lapse or live in utter impenitence. Our gospel is not a gospel of human achievement but of divine forgiveness and grace. To that gospel we are to bear witness and the loving reconciliation of Christian with Christian is a vital element in that witness. Sometimes our actions shout so loud that the gospel we are trying to

44

proclaim cannot be heard. It will not be surprising if the outsider is inattentive to our message of reconciliation at the cross if our church life seems to proclaim the opposite.

'They recognised that they had been with Jesus' (Acts 4:13) was first given as a comment on the boldness of Peter and John when on trial. But it is a principle that should be worked through in every contemporary contact between the Christian community and the world.

We live in an age when much of the contact has been lost. No more can we depend upon consistent religious education in our schools, and the trend suggests that this will continue to diminish. No more does every parent in the land seek a Christian minister to baptise the baby. I can recollect days in my curacy ministry when week after week there were children being baptised and even more mothers coming for that strange institution called 'churching'. It was almost superstition, but in a strange way it brought people into contact with the church at a vulnerable point in their lives. But all that has largely gone.

At the same time we must not minimise the opportunities of this kind of contact. Indeed, with so much less nominalism it is possible for the church to witness even more effectively to the real meaning of baptism and similar occasions. I have every sympathy with Christian ministers who practise infant baptism and yet have a very rigorous policy. On the other hand I am also very sympathetic to the point of view which wants to seize the opportunity rather than shut the door. Thankfully most churches now run preparation groups and give an opportunity for those who still wish for baptism to think through their vows seriously, and I can testify to the way the Lord can use this to draw parents who mean business to himself.

When the church does have this face-to-face encounter with the non-Christian who is moving in our direction it is vital that the manner of our ministry should commend Jesus. How easy it is to be so welcoming as to be soft or to be so strong for the truth as to be ungracious. We need to recognise that we are living in a world where there is much emptiness and where people are seeking for reality and purpose for living. I have lived to see the virtual death of any serious humanism. It has become obvious that the world is bankrupt of a philosophy which gives hope and meaning. The God-shaped whole at the centre of all of us needs to be filled and we must not betray our generation by refusing to offer clearly and joyfully the one message which can satisfy.

In this community encounter we are also aware of much loneliness. Many teenagers face the future with bleakness. Many young couples are being uprooted and on the move constantly, and older people feel that all around them the landmarks familiar from the past are going. Somewhere in between middle-aged people suffer from the uncertainties which lead to depression. In this context the church lives today. It can provide a community centre which can give spice and excitement to life which has often grown dull and stale. More often than not the first demonstration of the relevance of the gospel will be at this level.

Christians who show care have a unique opportunity to proclaim sensitively the gospel which engenders that care in them. It has been our happy experience that through playgroups for younger parents, groups for senior citizens, teenage fellowships and just the normal family life of the church we are given an opening for the gospel because we provide at the point of people's felt needs. We are privileged now to have facilities to enable us to do this in our church in Sheffield. In some situations it would be quite impossible and wrong to think in terms of the church owning the facilities, and there Christians must move into the secular environment to act as salt and light to provide that manpower which is all too often lacking. Christians ought to be motivated in service within the community, while never being content primarily with social concern. The apostle James reminds us that we cannot preach the gospel to those who have material needs unless first we show that we care to meet those needs. It is true not only of the needs of material proverty but of alienation and emptiness.

The minister or local Christian leader has a very special responsibility in all this. Increasingly the minister is not known and there are many reasons for this, not least the decline in the number of ordained ministers and the danger that with all the pressures upon us we are content to organise things from our home and are all too rarely seen around the place. It is too sick a joke to be very funny that so many people feel that ministers only appear on Sundays and special occasions. (I still wince with annoyance when I am reminded that Sunday is my 'busy day' and that Christmas is my 'busy period'). I foresee the danger of full-time ministry being at a distance from people. It would indeed be sad if spiritual help was given by some flying squad of ministers who entered an area, did their job and then disappeared. It has been the pride of the ministry that we are earthed in the local context, and that is vital, I believe, for effective ministry. In a very real way it was significant that people used to see the whole ministry of the church focused in the minister or the local church leader who was known and respected. In that sense the preaching ministry which is earthed in the locality is infinitely more demanding but infinitely more effective than an itinerant kind of ministry, valuable though that may be.

But it is the Christian community which encounters the world rather than any specific Christian leader. Indeed it is the witness of a community living together which is the heart of that testimony. Eclectic congregations are necessary in an imperfect world but I believe they make less impact than a local church which is seen not just when they gather for Sunday worship but in the total life of that district.

Because we live in an age of tragic conflict and division, the witness of Christian unity is absolutely vital. This involves the challenge of ecumenism. Sometimes I believe the denominational differences are much exaggerated and I am not convinced that many people are kept from faith because they see different denominations doing their own thing. But they may well be kept from faith when they see those denominations sniping at each other and claiming superiority. The situation in Northern Ireland, for example, is infinitely more complex than arrogant Englishmen often think. It has been my privilege to minister there regularly for over twenty years and I have come to love the place and its people. Christians there know as well as I that the tragic divisions in the church do not help in their witness. It is not a simple matter of Protestant versus Catholic, and we need to be so careful not to preach sermons to our brothers and sisters across the Irish Sea. This situation highlights the dangers of sectarian division, but whenever Christians are seen working and praying together it is in itself part of the gospel ministry and the message of hope.

I am always disturbed when I find Christians too readily marching behind slogans about the political problems of our world. I find the answers rather more complex than slogans allow. But I do believe that Christians should be seen as those who make their voice heard against evils such as apartheid in South Africa. I have personally found it impossible thus far to accept invitations to preach in South Africa because of a feeling that it would be very difficult to preach the gospel without reference to the political situation, and I have never felt that an outsider coming in on a special mission was the right person to do that. But our prayers and our concern should be all on behalf of the unity of races in that country. The Christian testimony is lost when we seek to gloss over evils such as apartheid. Yet it is so difficult to be consistent. We must as Christians oppose hatred and division wherever we find it, and we must be very ready to see the beam in our own eye first. It is easier to shout slogans at others than to put right the differences and bitternesses within our own communities.

We do not have to travel abroad to see great barriers which need to be destroyed by the gospel within the church community. I have noticed in my years of ministry the growing divide between the north and south in the UK, between those who have power and those who feel they have none. There may be no easy solution to this and the church is wise not to pretend to be politically expert. But we are called to be those who demonstrate that in Christ there is no barrier. It is not only denomination that has been destroyed in the unity that there is in Christ Jesus (Gal. 3:28).

One of the marks of the fatherhood of God is that he is no 'respecter of persons'. Too often the church has sadly failed at this level, as the apostle James is at pains to point out in his dynamic letter. I have always held it before myself as a very significant ideal in my ministry that I would treat all people alike, whatever their background or their gifts. There has been failure enough, but I never lose sight of this ideal of the reality of our gospel and of our God.

Surely our Lord has this partly in mind when he prays in his great prayer in John chapter 17 that the church might be one 'that the world may believe' (verse 21). The demonstration of Christian unity at every level has an evangelistic note about it. It does not mean that Christians should seek after unity at the expense of truth. The apostle Paul who battles for the unity of the church also speaks very strongly against any idea of tolerance of another gospel. In Galatians 1:6-9 he uses the most forceful language against all who would proclaim a different gospel. There will be those who name the name of Christ with whom Bible-believing Christians can never be at one. Tolerance is not the supreme virtue. But equally, Christians must learn that secondary issues can be forgotten in the pursuit of true brotherly unity which reflects the character of God and the unifying power of the gospel.

I have noticed in my years of ministry that the divides are not primarily denominational these days, but more to do with styles of worship and of expression. Behind all these there may be a theological basis, but often it is at a more superficial level that we divide. Strangely enough that can make the divide more painful and the way to healing more difficult. In some ways this ties in with the whole 'charismatic' movement and the attempts in the last decade to heal the divisions in the church. On the one hand there are wild claims, often unsubstantiated, which quite rightly frighten those who take the word of God seriously. There is too much stress on experience and an underplaying of the doctrines of Scripture. On the other hand there are often unfounded fears and statements based on rumour rather than on fact. Happily some of us have discovered that there is a place of meeting in the service of the Lord. I believe that the world is impressed when they see Christians who have honest differences of opinion working together amicably. What in the world would lead to confrontation should within the Christian community lead to creative tension. The words are easy to write but demanding in their reality.

In my more recent experience of sharing in Mission England-Sheffield this was one of the greatest blessings. Long before we saw thousands of people added to the kingdom we discovered that we could work together across that charismatic divide. It is equally true that once the moment of united evangelism has gone the differences can easily begin to rear their ugly heads again. Satan is not silly and he knows when to make his thrust. Each Christian must have a dedication to be honest before God, to seek for a unity within the gospel which will commend Jesus through his church to the world and not to be an agent of unnecessary conflict and confrontation.

The evangelical has a specific contribution to make and a particular problem. It is always a vexed question as to whether all true Christians should be evangelicals. It is certainly true that many devout Christians seem not to rejoice in that label. Those of us who do and who would like to see the extension of that beloved word are often on the horns of a dilemma. Because we take very seriously our convictions about the truths of Scripture it is very easy to become rigid and unloving. It is easy to see the difference in theory between misguided views and those who hold them. It is much more difficult in practice to battle for the truth and still to love those who seem either to deny it or to be very happy to accommodate every kind of view.

Certainly evangelicals must be sure that they are fighting true biblical battles and not just those of their own making. Some battles have been fought and won and are now irrelevant. But some remain and it is my personal conviction that the battle for the final authority of Scripture is certainly still being waged. There are many on the periphery of evangelicalism who seem to sit lightly by the cardinal doctrine of the Scripture's inspiration. 2 Timothy 3:16 is very clear in its statement and I believe that we dare not move from this conviction that 'all scripture is inspired by God'. That verb means 'God-breathed'. Anything less puts many of our Christian doctrines at risk and even denies the reality of much of our spiritual experience.

In the climate of today, when this battle is being refought, it is very tempting to raise once more the vision of a united evangelical church gathered from all denominations. I was not very much involved in church affairs when this battle was fought out with Dr Martyn Lloyd Jones on the one hand and Rev John Stott on the other debating whether or not evangelical Christians should leave their denominations and become a united church. I believe that we were right not to seek to bring all evangelical Christians together in one structure at that time and I believe that it is still the purpose of God that we should go on seeking to infiltrate denominations or indeed to remind them of the scriptural basis on which most of them still profess. What we dare not do is to become more Anglican or Methodist or Baptist than evangelical. I have no hesitation in saying that I am closer in fellowship to non-Anglican evangelicals than to non-evangelical Anglicans because we hold on to the same truths and our areas of disagreements are in matters that are not central to the gospel. But many would not share my conviction, and I believe that here is the battleground for the future.

Other people have defined an evangelical far more

effectively than I can ever begin to do. But an evangelical is certainly a gospel person, a Bible-centred person, and a person who glories in the great Reformation doctrine of justification by grace through faith alone. He will bring all other insights under the scrutiny of Scripture. The evangelical should be open always to what the Spirit of God is saying through the Word of God, but he will always be suspicious of any new truth that does not have its anchorage in Scripture. One of the favourite phrases of the day is that Christians should be open. That is only half the truth. In some ways we are closed in to the revelation of God in the Bible. God certainly still speaks but he does not contradict himself.

There is one other stage on which the drama of God's truth is being enacted through the church. This is the world stage, and in a small way I have been privileged to see something of the gospel transcending national and cultural barriers. It was my privilege to be Chairman of SUM Fellowship when the Church of Christ in Nigeria became completely independent. This was not without its pains and traumas. No child comes to birth without some travail, but it was a wonderful experience of seeing God at work and enjoying something of the fulfilment of the work of missionaries over many decades. To be able to see a church growing to maturity, which includes an ability to keep a loving relationship with its old mother church, is another demonstration of the reality of God's grace and love. In other ways too the churches in the Third World, with their growth in many places and their vitality which often makes us seem rather stale and dull, are the demonstration of the reality of God at work. It may be very humbling for western Christians to recognise that we are now very much in a minority. It would certainly be foolish to suggest that everything in the church in the Third World is an example to us and a standing rebuke to our lack of life. We still have much to offer and many churches in many parts of the world are in dire danger of losing their momentum because of lack of teaching in depth. Yet the thrilling growth of churches in our day is a drama that makes biblical truth live afresh.

One of the significant elements in the New Testament when considering the unity of the church was Paul's deep concern to encourage Christians to give towards the poor church in Jerusalem, not only in a fit of compassion but as a demonstration of theological truth. Here in a vivid way he saw that the dynamic unity of the church was practical and a challenge to the world. One of the most remarkable events in my ministerial lifetime has been the creation and growth of Tear Fund, with its balanced emphasis on reaching the whole man in his physical, social and spiritual need throughout the world. The response to Tear Fund has been a great encouragement, for here Christians have been demonstrating that they do care deeply about man in his wholeness. I see it as a kind of parable. There can be no doubt that our world has become very conscious of the needs of suffering humanity and I believe that to be God at work, even though many of his agents would not call themselves Christians. The church must add the extra spiritual dimension because we are dealing with a man who does not live by bread alone.

All this dramatic presentation through the church can only be effective in the world when the church in its home environment is united, relevant and alive. Satan knows that he will spoil the work of the church best by getting at Christians in their worship. It is there that we need to give attention at this point in our thinking. For, although the world does not normally see us at worship, it is what we are there that we really are. We shall never present the true picture of the gospel outside unless we are right inside.

54

5

The Church at Worship

Words have their vogue in the Christian world as elsewhere. One of the fashionable words of today is 'worship'. No one should cavil at the resurgence of that great word. But unfortunately it is often used in a very limited sense. For example, the worship in a service is seen as distinct from the preaching, and yet very central to worship is the listening to God's word. On the other hand a good old-fashioned phrase in the liturgy reminds us that we do worship God in the offering. I believe that the giving of our money in the collection plate, however it may be done these days, is in itself an act of worship, since the word in its English form reminds us that we are telling God what he is worth.

Worship does not stop at the church door and Paul reminds us in Romans 12:1-2 that the offering of our bodies as a living sacrifice is our 'spiritual worship'. What happens within the building we rather superficially call 'the church' on Sundays must always be closely linked with what happens in the world during the rest of the week. The more our churches symbolically demonstrate that they are part of the community the better. There is an inevitable rhythm about the Christian life. It is all a matter of coming and going. We shall be very ineffective if we do not make time to come together, and our church worship will be utterly fruitless if it does not issue in a more effective going into the world.

There is a marvellous juxtaposition in Luke chapter 10 where Jesus tells the story of the Good Samaritan to a lawyer who just wanted to debate, and the final challenge is to 'go and do'. Then immediately there is the story of Martha and Mary, where Martha is gently rebuked because she is so busy in service that she does not sit at the master's feet and listen. Pietists need to be reminded that their gospel is meant for the world and activists should always be alert to the danger of a Christian rush in the energy of the flesh. We all need to meet to worship and in worship we must give God the best.

It is very easy to be obsessed by church buildings, and one of the problems of the church today is the edifices which have been handed down to us. Sometimes they are the greatest impediment to progress in the spiritual life of our nation. A good friend of mine assured me that he had informed his congregation that if anyone saw the church on fire they must not ring the fire brigade for at least fifteen minutes, so that it could get a good hold! He was not being an iconoclast, but just an exasperated minister of the gospel.

As we have seen before, the 1662 Common Book of Prayer defines the church as a 'congregation of faithful men in which the pure word of God is preached and the sacraments are duly ministered'. The centrality of the word and its preaching is very clear. But there are always problems of emphasis. In some churches where the preaching is the significant element it is tempting to think of the rest of the service as mere preliminaries, and that word is often used. I am grateful to have been trained in my curacy days by a man who loved the beauty of worship and emphasised the importance of giving as much time in preparing prayers and hymns as in the preparation of the address. I cannot pretend always to have heeded that advice but I believe it was a formative influence in my ministry and a very valuable corrective.

On the other hand we are in greater danger today of going to the other extreme. Praise is the order of the day, and it is suggested that if praise is really heartfelt then preaching is almost superfluous. We shall very soon reap the whirlwind if we allow congregations to be content with an orgy of singing and nothing more. Very quickly such praise becomes mindless, and the apostle Paul is at pains always to point out that worship must be with the mind as well as with the Spirit.

Sacraments are significant alongside the preaching of the Word, and it has been a significant revolution in recent years that evangelicals have been renewed in their love for the Lord's Supper. Clearly the New Testament makes the breaking of bread a very high priority. For many people the Lord is made known in that breaking of bread, with the proviso that it becomes no magical rite but is an outward and visible manifestation of the truth of the gospel which is being verbally proclaimed. It is always easy for any movement of God to become twisted by man. Nowhere is that tragedy more evident than in the fact that this glorious sacrament of Christian unity has often become the focal point of division.

While avoiding the danger of dependence upon externals we must be aware that God speaks to us not just through words heard but through the visual symbol. This is the purpose of the sacraments of Baptism and Holy Communion. We are also today renewing our belief that there is a value in the use of art and drama in proclaiming the gospel. These must be subservient to the word of God and aids to its proclamation. But for many people they enrich the message greatly.

In practice the balance of word and sacrament is not easy. Some evangelical Christians would want to emphasise that the main worship service of each Sunday should be a Communion service, and they would plead a biblical precedent. But there are difficulties, not least in the desire to reach the outsider with the gospel message. I can rejoice on occasions when I have known people come to Christ through the service of Communion. But I believe that we do have practical problems making the outsider feel welcome if at every service there is the breaking of bread, which excludes him. Equally I believe that we have not worked out the place of children at the Communion rail. The common practice of laying on hands of blessing has much to commend it, although is not altogether popular with older children. Their enthusiasm for it does not very often equal that of their parents.

People's experiences will vary but for many of us some of the highlights of our experience will be linked with Communion. I have never grown tired of the moving experience at the Keswick Convention when the thousands in utter silence break bread together and then finish with a great hymn of anticipation of the Lord's return. Without being trite, I must say it is very often a lovely foretaste of heaven. Equally, I have been deeply moved by a tiny Communion service in a home. I well remember the testimony of a Christian colleague now in heaven who had been in a Japanese prisoner of war camp and spoke of the most moving Communion service he had ever attended. None of the right elements were present – there was no bread, no wine, no minister and no church building. But a group of Christians soon to be parted, many of them en route for heaven, met to break rice-mould and pour cold tea and to remember Jesus. My friend could never speak of the event without being visibly moved. It is no bad thing when worship is so Spirit-filled that we cannot recollect the occasion without tears.

To be together is part of the value of worship. Hebrews 10:25 is a solemn warning to Christians not to neglect meeting together. Apparently even in those early days, either through fear or laziness or a wrong kind of theology, Christians were neglecting the corporate element in their faith. A family is still a family even when far apart, but clearly it becomes more united when it meets together. The adage is as true in church life as in ordinary family life: 'the family that prays together stays together'.

The concept of the church as the family of God has become more popular in recent years. There is much to commend it, since it underlines that we do not meet in a church building as a collection of individuals just doing their own thing. We meet to demonstrate our family love for each other and for our Father in heaven. The wild modern concept in some parts of the world of a church where you may plug into worship while still sitting in your own car is a denial of what worship means. It is wonderful that with our modern technology Christians who are inevitably cut off from worship because of illnesss or old age can receive something of the atmosphere through radio and television. But this is at best a substitute for times of emergency.

There are limitations to the idea of a family church. While the fellowship must be a family of families, it must be very much a family which transcends families, and therefore the single, widowed and divorced should not feel left out of it. The popularity of family services in recent years has had its good points but it has certainly has some unhelpful ramifications. Sometimes the lonely person is made to feel more lonely, the one without an earthly family made actually more bereft than ever. It is equally true that with the emphasis on family services the preaching has often become child-centred and the depth has gone. In many ways the superficiality which characterises much of Christian worship today has been encouraged by this kind of activity within the church. But the concept of the family at worship is absolutely biblical and needs to be emphasised.

Encouragement should be a hallmark of Christians at worship. 1 Thessalonians 5:11 is in itself a challenge to be a church where Christians encourage and build up one another. Herein lies a problem for larger churches. It is good to be growing and there is a very real place for large congregations, with the inspiration they provide. We should not proclaim that 'small is beautiful' as a means of rationalising our failure. But in larger congregations there need to be smaller groups meeting so that people can help and share with one another. Also it is vital that church services should include some opportunity for personal greeting or meeting over lunch or coffee.

There is a challenge to different temperaments. It is easy to hide behind shyness and to assume that because I find it difficult to go into a group, therefore the Lord does not mean me to do so. The Bible is full of challenges to trust him, to launch out into the deep and not to be defeated by temperament. Paul had to ginger up Timothy, a timid man, to be ready to overcome in the Spirit his natural temperamental problem. Equally, the extrovert has the problem that he or she may meet a lot of people in a shallow manner but never talk in depth to anyone. In the beautiful economy of God within the Body of Christ he has placed both introverts and extroverts. So there should be a balance of those who can break the ice easily and those who can gently and in depth get to know a few people well and help them along the way.

Within that family context of the church we grow together. But there is no substitute for the importance of the nuclear family in the plan of God. The Bible has as much to say about the ordinary human family as it does about the family of the church. The work of the church does not mean that parents no longer have the responsibility to bring up their children in the way of the Lord. For a very few community living may take the place of the nuclear family. But this is not the norm. The norm is that nuclear family which so often Satan wants to attack and destroy. The church family should encourage the earthly family to be more united in Christ.

One of the problems about being a church family is created by the very shape of our buildings. Some of the most beautiful ancient churches seem to have a strange theological justification. The large part of the area of the church is at the east end, often cut off by a screen from the main body of the congregation. It all seems to highlight what the 'professionals' are doing up there, leading the people down there. The exaltation of Communion is not in itself wrong, but we should seek as practically as possible to have the Communion table out in the body of the church and seen to be not a place where a priest does his thing but a table where the people of the Lord gather together to share in a family meal. Even a dominant pulpit has theological problems. It is good to emphasise the centrality of the word preached and read, but even that can accentuate the idea of a one-man ministry, which has been such a stumbling block. The ideal is a church which is seen to be in the round and where there is flexibility for movement. We need to be careful not to be under the dictate of architecture.

It is our own personal testimony in the church where I minister in Sheffield that church extension and alteration has helped in our worship. Even the building of a new church hall, lounge and youth centre next door also has its significant message. The church does not exist only on Sundays, and the community buildings demonstrate the continuing life of the church within the neighbourhood seven days a week. Not least within the church building we need to ensure that all people can see and hear. People cannot believe if they have never heard and they cannot hear if the preacher is not able to throw his voice or the amplification never works. One of the problems of involving more and more people is that of keeping the simple standard of reading and speaking at the right level. The things that inhibit the Spirit are sometimes very simple, practical things.

As well as the shape of the building the structure of our services also sometimes militate against family worship. It is important to have order, and indeed from the first chapter of Scripture the Spirit brought order and form. People feel more relaxed when there is a sense of order and they know what to expect. Nor is it possible or wise to make every act of worship different and unique. But there is the danger of dull repetition; there is the possibility of knowing exactly what is going to happen and therefore never allowing room for the Spirit to move or anything out of the ordinary to occur. There needs to be a sense of anticipation that anything might happen when we meet as the family of God. The balance is there in Paul's writing very clearly. 1 Corinthians chapter 14 is all on this theme, that there should be flexibility and participation from people within the congregation. But there needs to be order, authority and firmness. Our worship should mirror the reality of the creation. In creation we have a God of order who is also a God of delightful diversity. So it should be with the God of redemption. There is purpose and pattern, but there is also a richness which should characterise Christians when they meet together to worship the God who is both Creator and Redeemer.

As might be expected in our day, the element of praise and thanksgiving in worship has become more significant and its pursuit more uninhibited. As ever there are gains and losses in this movement. It has been a joy to reinstate praise where once Christians were very formal in their worship and much happier at intercessory prayer than praise. Sadly, now the wheel has gone very much full circle and in some groups it is far easier to get people to sing choruses of praise than to intercede. The old-fashioned prayer meeting may have had its limitations and was easily caricatured but it was the powerhouse for so much effective Christian ministry and will be lost at our peril.

But we do rejoice that praise has come to the fore. In the process we have rediscovered the Psalms and their wealth of expression of Christian devotion. Not only do they give us the springboard for much singing of praise but also a great treasury for those who find praise hard in the midst of depression and doubt. Alongside the rediscovery of large tracts of the Old Testament, we are also writing hymns again. Inevitably when there is a resurgence of this kind of composition there is an extraordinary mixture of gem and rubbish. But it has ever been so, and it would not be difficult to produce a whole library of very dubious hymns from the Victorian era, some of which we sing without pondering the words. Whenever spiritual revival happens, hymn singing is never far away. So it was in Wesley's day and happily so it is today. Much of it will be ephemeral, and that is excellent. In some ways we write for today and care not for tomorrow.

Equally joyful is the reinstatement of other instruments of music apart from the organ. It is strange how the organ now has a sort of sanctity attached to it and some people who cherish the past shake heads in sadness at the advent of the guitar and orchestra. But in fact the organ is a fairly modern accompaniment of worship, and we must be happy that many more people with musical gifts can now help us in our praise. The church which refuses to accept these modern aids is missing a great deal.

But there is a joy in catholicity of praise. I am still sufficiently an Anglican of the old order to enjoy singing Psalms and canticles to chants. These become more difficult as more and more of traditional Anglican church choirs fade away. But I do believe that they provide a useful variation on the kind of singing and music. Certainly we should not become so sold on modern choruses that we forget the great wealth of the past. Perhaps never again will we have hymns so chock-full of theology as those of Charles Wesley. As with Christian literature, we needlessly make ourselves paupers if we only concentrate on the contemporary.

There is also a danger in some of our modern praise items that there is an unhealthy repetition and, from one who is not a musician of any sort, a kind of music which lacks the vigour and strength of some of the music from the past. We often indicate the kind of Christianity we cherish by the kind of music we sing, and the image of today does not always demonstrate virility but rather a slightly sickly-sweet introspective sentimentality. But there are many gains, and some of the most lovely of the modern songs are simply Scripture set to music. I have a personal affection for the objective hymns of every age rather than the subjective ones telling the Lord how I feel. Perhaps this is because I can be more sure when I sing the truths that never change, and my feelings do change. But there is a place for the love songs within the Christian praise repertoire.

There was an age which encouraged people in church, whether the minister or congregation, to remain fairly anonymous and to hide their personalities so that they did not obtrude in worship. Now we have moved very far away and often we are encouraged to use our whole body in worship. There is nothing strange about this. The Psalmist certainly encouraged us to use all that we are and have in our worship. The preacher who does not use his limbs tends to be somewhat dull to the audience. There is an expressiveness about the use of the hands which helps and I so cannot believe that there is something displeasing to God about those who feel it right to lift up hands in worship. On the other hand there is the awful danger of stereotype, of a foolish parading of ourselves in strange gyrations before our fellow men. We need to be quite sure that we are expressing ourselves to God and not to others. Inevitably there will always be a limitation to what we do in public worship because we are mindful that we are not alone and others may well be distracted from worshipping because of the way we perform. As one who enjoys moving his body in singing hymns with enthusiasm, I have never felt any need to lift up my hands to help me and I have sometimes been a slightly bemused spectator of those who do. I must one day discover why it is a certain kind of hymn which seems to encourage this and not another. It is not simply a matter of praise or prayer, but seems to have something to do with the stable from which the hymn or chorus comes. On the other hand those who do not find this kind of manual worship helpful must be careful not to be legalistic and to assume all kinds of wrong motives in those who do.

Within this context there is the whole question of the use of sacred dance. It is interesting to ponder how far we have moved in a short time. As a young man I cannot conceive that any church in the British Isles would have thought seriously of the place of dance in worship. I still find it perplexing and I am not very convinced when King David is cited as the originator and ultimate sanction of this kind of dance. His jig before the ark is not altogether seen as something to be commended. The New Testament is significantly silent on the subject. Yet we from time to time in our own church have used dance within worship and, although it is inevitably divisive, there are those who profess to have been greatly uplifted and helped by it. Beautifully and reverently done, it can express a sense of joy before the God of Creation and indeed, well executed, has a message in itself. But I fear that we are pushing the bounds back dangerously and the occasional sight of a whole congregation given over to spontaneous dance before the Lord has not to me been edifying. It would seem to go against the whole concept of corporate worship by its intrusion of our own personal feelings within the Body of Christ.

Paul keeps on reminding us that worship must always be with the mind and with the Spirit. It may well have been that much worship was far too cerebral in the past, depending almost completely on an intellectual response to the truth expounded. It ought to be the case that the word of God read and proclaimed demands an immediate response of praise and thanksgiving, although it may also call for moments of silence and penitence. We must be careful in our reinstatement of praise not to go overboard and imagine that the worth of a service must always be seen in vigorous enthusiasm.

Moreover the ultimate test of the power of the word of God is not how we behave in church but how we behave day by day. I fear that some imagine that the Lord looks down from heaven on our worship participation more than he does on our daily living. The Old Testament prophets would have had something fairly severe to say to those who felt that way. But corporate worship should enable us the better to live and, by our response to the God who speaks to us strengthen us, to serve him better day by day.

It is true that meeting together imposes certain limitations. It is 'common prayer', and we exercise some restraint because of that. Even more is it true, however, that corporate worship should provide a great uplift. The battle can be hard and sometimes the spirit can become very much battered by the world, the flesh and the devil. To meet together for praise and worship should lift us up and send us back with renewed determination to live for Christ and to obey his Word in the world.

At the heart of all worship must be the preaching and hearing of the Word of God. Without this, acts of worship can very rapidly become meaningless repetition. As a preacher I am happiest when the Word of God comes as the climax of a service and all else builds up to it. There are arguments for having the sermon earlier within the act of worship so there can be a proper response of praise and prayer. Perhaps more pointedly there is value in hearing the sermon immediately before being sent out into the world to obey. The primary challenge of a sermon is to go and do, and every preacher must prayerfully consider in preparation what is the purpose of the sermon and what response he expects. Preaching in the New Testament calls for a verdict. Thus our Lord ended the sermon on the mount with the parable of the two houses and the call to hear the Word of God and do it. Peter on the day of Pentecost was more than ready for the audience asking what they ought to do with their sense of conviction. To that end in the Spirit he had been preaching. In that way it is helpful if, after quiet reflection, those who have heard the word go back into the world and seek to carry out its implications.

Preacher and hearer alike should expect that each sermon is in itself an act of God. There will be the creative blend of objective truth expounded from Scripture with all its authority and a subjective experience of the promptings of the Spirit calling for appropriate action. Even in Old Testament days there are parallels, as in Nehemiah chapter 8 where Ezra the scribe preaches and there is a reponse from the people of Israel, aware of their sins and eager to make amends. I believe that we are living in a situation where often unconciously people are crying for a word from the Lord and often come in vain to worship. The failure for that word to reach people is sometimes because the preacher has lost confidence in Scripture and sometimes because the faithful expositor does not relate the truths of Scripture to the world of today. We must be earthed at both ends. Without Scripture our comments are banal; without our feet firmly on the ground of contemporary reality we are just becoming biblical experts. Our aim is not to produce a congregation who simply know the Bible but a congregation who know the Lord and obey him.

The richness of Scripture is there to enable us to bring out a challenge for every situation. The apostle Paul would engage in dialogue when he went from place to place, taking Old Testament scriptures relating them to Jesus and applying them often under great hostility to the people in the synagogue or elsewhere. Much effective preaching should happen outside the public acts of worship, particularly in the realm of outreach. We need men and women who actually know how to relate the eternal truths within the secular context.

But for the people of God there is the need for systematic teaching in order that they might grow and relate their faith to everyday life. The preacher must not assume that he is an expert in politics or in medicine or in any of the other disciplines. It is the task of each member of the congregation to relate the thrust of the word of God to their particular context. The preacher must help the faithful to understand what God is saying in his Word. It is significant that after the church at Antioch had come alive Barnabas saw the need for some foundation teaching, so he brought the apostle Paul for his first great ministry, and for a whole year the faithful were taught and edified. It could be argued that the greatest need of our day is for that kind of teaching and that much worship has become subjective and thin because the sermon has all too often been diminished in value.

To achieve this object of enabling the people of God to hear the Word of God there needs to be a regular teaching sequence. It is vital that people should be instructed in the whole counsel of God and not just the particular themes and fads of their minister. I have always sought to give blocks of teaching based either on individual books of the Bible or on themes or characters. Sometimes it is valuable to look at the Lord's Prayer or the Ten Commandments or the Sermon on the Mount or the Creed. It is wise to ring the changes and not to make the series too long. It is possible to be too minute in some examination of Scripture and to spend far too long on one particular aspect of it. But a greater danger is lack of continuity and I believe a congregation will be the healthier if there is a structured teaching ministry. Also the preacher himself will be kept from going stale with this kind of discipline.

Of course, the preacher needs to be sensitive to what is happening in the world and to be a person of imagination. Events in the world outside colour the minds of people as they come to worship, and it is foolish to ignore them. From time to time some major event may call for a last minute change of sermon. More likely, by the gracious providence of God, the theme already planned for the day can well incorporate some reference to that particular event which is on people's minds. At the same time it is vital that the agenda for our sermons should be dictated not by the world and its ideas nor even by the congregation and its desires but by the balance of Scripture. There are many issues which I would not have dared to preach unless they came in the sequence of teaching.

Here I believe lies the key to making an act of worship something to be anticipated with eagerness and not gone through as a grim obligation. Ultimately I believe the quality of the preaching will be the final factor in making worship alive.

The particular challenge of preaching within worship is that inevitably there will be a glorious cross-section of levels of Christian maturity, and each one comes needing to hear a word from the Lord. Without the miracle of the Spirit at work this would be a sheer impossibility. We are wise to remember that there is a need for groups to meet together with a common interest or a particular level of understanding. The recent popularity of nurture groups or basics groups is altogether a good thing in that it encourages young Christians to meet together to receive the milk of the word. It only becomes tragic when some people never get beyond the basics stage and are content to remain in the kindergarten. Equally it is important to to have Bible teaching for young people at a particular age, and obviously the children's groups are essential if the younger folk are to hear the Lord speaking at a level they can understand.

Yet there is a special value in the exhortation that comes to the whole congregation gathered together. As part of worship there is the atmosphere of being consciously in the presence of God and having been prepared through different facets of worship to go that stage further in our Christian experience as the Lord speaks to us. There is always a two-way traffic in preaching Naturally the preacher must give much time in preparation and give it that priority which alone will safeguard the sermon against the assaults of a busy diary. Ultimately no amount of efficient administration can take the place of waiting upon the Lord to hear what he would say through his word and carefully preparing that Word. Paul's exhortation to Timothy in 2 Timothy 4:2 remains the classic challenge to the preacher: 'preach the word, be urgent in season and out of season, convince, rebuke and exhort, be unfailing in patience and in teaching'. Paul goes on to remind Timothy that it is all the more necessary because of the false teaching that is around, and that certainly is the clarion-call of today. Those of us who love God's Word and believe in its purity must be bold and imaginative in its proclamation. The truth needs to be heard loud and clear.

Of course, the other side of the two-way traffic in preaching is the need of the congregation to prepare prayerfully. There is a grace of listening and there is a discipline in taking God's Word seriously. For some people it means taking notes in the sermon in order to help concentration. For others it may mean following a series through by listening to taped sermons. Supremely it calls for an attitude of mind which expects that God will speak. In many cases where there is this thirst for the truth from the congregation a preacher can be lifted to a new level. It is my testimony, having preached in very many places to very many different congregations, that it is highly important to come to a prayerfully prepared people. I am happy to confess that this is my normal lot in my own congregation, and it makes preaching a sheer delight. But prayer alone can make preaching live.

Prayer is much more than intercession and an older generation of evangelical Christian sometimes forgot this. I have always found it easier to ask than to thank and praise and I am therefore grateful for the modern reminder of the primacy of praise and thanksgiving. But we must not forget that we are counselled by our Lord to ask and that intercession is a duty of the whole church gathered together in worship.

The church is seen in the New Testament as continuing two functions from the Old Testament. There is the prophetic ministry which proclaims the truth of God and there is the priestly ministry which brings people to God in prayer, just as the Old Testament priest of Aaron's line would bear the names of the children of Israel on his breast before God. Thus whenever he entered into the holy place he was symbolically representing them and remembering them. In the Christian era the church *is* – not *has* – a priesthood. It is the priesthood of all believers and together we are called to intercede for others, often for those who do not intercede for themselves.

Another Old Testament picture is fulfilled in the church at prayer, and that is the solemn analogy of the watchman who has a responsibility to keep watch and to warn. In that ministry there is both the proclamation note and the note of prayerful waiting upon the Lord. In that spirit Abraham prayed his most remarkable prayer in Genesis chapter 18 when, knowing his position as a friend of God, he interceded for Sodom and for his nephew Lot within it. It can be a very painful ministry and goes way beyond what happens in church, but there is a special place for united intercession as we act as priests before God.

We are urged in Scripture to pray for those in authority, and that is a unique responsibility of Christian citizens. We are also of course encouraged to pray for the church and for individuals. One of the joys of extending the congregational participation in worship is to involve more people openly in intercession. Many ministers frankly do not have or give time for preparing the prayers as they should, and inevitably they are based upon the ritual of a book or on one person's extempore prayers. To involve many more people extends the involvement in intercession and often gives deeper richness to it. My experience has been that lay people of all ages have lifted us very close to heaven in the quality of their prayers within church. There is also the value of silent prayer, when individuals within the congregation are encouraged to pray together, interceding in the silence for some particular issue. We need to be realistic in our use of periods of silence, but this is certainly an element of intercession which should not be forgotten. We can be too noisy in church.

Naturally, prayer in church is no substitute for the private devotions of the individual Christian. These demand daily discipline and order. I have never found it easy to be inspired in my own private prayers, but I do believe that God nevertheless honours the prayers that come rather prosaically and more out of a sense of duty than delight. I may envy those who spend long hours in prayer with great joy before the Lord, but it may be that this will never be my lot and I may in this way be able to relate to the average Christian who often battles in prayer.

I believe that one of the aids the Lord gives us in our private prayers is prayer with others. Smaller prayer groups and prayer meetings can be a great inspiration. My experience is that the person who misuses prayer meetings with too many or excessively long prayers is very much an exception and that there is encouragement in hearing people of all ages, however haltingly, bring their problems before the Lord. When the design of the church building allows it there is a value in small groups even within public worship. But there needs to be a caution here, as there will always be those in church with no experience of open prayer and indeed some non-Christians and new Christians. We need to be sure we minimise the embarrassment caused to such people. Perhaps it would be wise to restrict this kind of praying to groups where people have specifically and positively come for that purpose. On the other hand, though, sometimes an embarrassment can challenge a person to action.

There is another caution that is equally more important to sound. There is a very thin line between mentioning people and their needs for prayer and discussing them in gossip-fashion around the parish. No church will have escaped this problem and every minister from time to time will have the agony of trying to sort out some mistake at this level. Where there are no prayer groups and where there is no sharing of individual or personal problems this will not arise, but a church without that provision would be poor indeed. We need as Christians to be very careful before the Lord that we talk about people's problems to the Lord rather than to one another. When we ask for the prayers of others we need to be extremely careful in the way in which we convey our information. It is one of the problems of a living church that the kind of thing which brings praying to life can also be used by Satan to bring gossip to the fore. There is an unhealthy sharing which is counter-productive. The intense group which demands every individual to bare his or her soul at each moment is not in the New Testament pattern. We are encouraged to share our problems and confess our sins to one another, but we are certainly not encouraged to make this into a kind of ritual which can often be very superficial.

Two kinds of praying have become common in recent years which again evoke joy and warning. Happily we have rediscovered that God is a God who heals and the healing service has become quite common in many churches. Inevitably this will be a personal matter. All Christians must accept that God is sovereign and that he chooses sometimes to heal and sometimes not to heal. We must never restrict him to the normal ways of science and medicine. There are enough encouragements in the New Testament to share in this healing ministry, not least in the letter of James, who advises us to call the elders to anoint the sick person with oil. However, this is an area where there is much misunderstanding and where there can be great hurt when promises are made which cannot be assured. It is very much a matter of personal counsel and I believe that such prayer for healing is far better accomplished within a small, caring, private group rather than before the public gaze of the congregation. Some Christian groups believe that there is a special efficacy in much public laying on of hands, especially around the Communion table. I fear that sometimes this places the emphasis more on the prayer for healing than the central act of Communion, and I would always opt to encourage prayer for healing to be done in the kind of privacy where a person can be well prepared for whatever the Lord might be pleased to do, whether in physical healing or in a new enabling to face the continued suffering which God in his sovereignty allows.

The other area of public prayer which is increasingly common is the laying on of hands for commissioning. This can be a very moving occasion when missionaries are being sent out or people are going out from one church to serve in another part of this country or when those are being commissioned who have a special task within the life of the church. This is a development of the pattern of ordination and helps people to see that the laity have their own commissioning for their particular tasks. In my own experience, almost every time this has been very significant. Here the act ought to be public, so that the whole church is involved as in the New Testament, where the whole church sent out Paul and Barnabas on the first overseas missionary enterprise (Acts 13:3).

The only snare here is that somewhere a line has to be drawn, but it is difficult to know where that particular line should be. It would be possible to argue for a commissioning service for virtually every task within the church, but then it would cease to have meaning. However, here is one area where the whole church meeting together is committed prayerfully to a particular individual or group so that they may go with the blessing of the whole fellowship.

One of the dangers of prayer within the local church is that it can become too parochial. I recollect speaking at a college chapel Communion service and alternating between being very moved and rather exasperated through the rather long free intercessions. It was moving in that so many took part and the smallest problem of the individual or college was noted. But we almost forgot the world outside! It seemed as if we expected the whole of the direction of the Almighty to be upon this small community, and there was no sense of being part of the wider body of Christ. We need to beware of this. My experience within our own church community has been that to interview people who come from other parts of the country or abroad helps to focus our attention beyond ourselves. Intercessions need to be wide as well as deeply intimate.

Here is the church playing its priestly role within the community. The encouragement of the New Testament is that when we begin to pray corporately something begins to happen. Supremely it can often happen within us and effective intercession can be a very powerful weapon for the Spirit to use right here immediately where we are praying. Thus Nehemiah prayed for Jerusalem and found himself being challenged to serve.

The house of God should be the place where things are always likely to happen, amid an air of excitement and anticipation. It was in the temple that Isaiah had the vision in which he heard the Lord inviting him and where he made his own response: 'Here am I! Send me'. (Is. 7:8). In the days of our Lord's ministry, when he was regularly at the synagogue, there were always likely to be memorable events. People were healed within the synagogue when Jesus appeared and divisions were caused by his teaching. The least we can do is to ensure prayerfully that the church is not boringly predictable. The total ministry of our worship should lead to a response from people there and then, with ramifications which will follow. Here is the opportunity for evangelism and, not just in the special services, we ought to expect people to be born again of the Spirit through our worship. Here too the challenge to service will find an echoing response. It is worthwhile to remember, however, that the response within the service does not necessarily mean much. The

77

proof will come when we are out of the church door and making practical the response of the heart. Paul reminds us that our spiritual worship is to present our bodies as living sacrifices. The weekly reminder of what that means should transform not just one day but all seven days of the week.

There is something very significant about the receiving of people's gifts of money within worship. Paul certainly sets us an example in 1 Corinthians 16:2. In our very different age, with complex bank accounts and credit cards, it is easy to lose the significance of the offering. There is nothing magical about putting cash in a collection plate rather than having a banker's order. But something is being lost, and certainly those who give rather more impersonally must be as careful as possible to ensure that the giving is systematic and sacrificial. I still have this old fashioned streak in me which believes that there is a value in making my financial offering within the service as a symbol of the whole of my possessions belonging to God. Certainly the New Testament encourages us to see this as a very vital part of our worship. Just as Paul had a crusade for giving to the poor in Jerusalem, so there must be a constant crusade today to encourage Christian people to be committed in their giving and to make it a cheerful response to the One who gave all for us.

There is always a rhythm in worship, with God taking the initiative and speaking to us, followed by our response to that voice. This is most obviously seen in the Communion service, where all focuses on God offering himself to us before we consciously give ourselves back to him as a living sacrifice. There is also a rhythm in our public worship of turning away from the business of the world to God so that we might go back into it refreshed and renewed. Despite the beauty of the old churches with their stained-glass windows and rather darkened interiors, a better environment is a light church with clear windows, so that the world outside is visible even as we worship. I am so delighted that in our newly-extended church we have this kind of pattern. It may be somewhat distracting occasionally to view some of the antics going on outside the church windows, but it is much more helpful to realise that we are not cut off from the world, a people apart. We are part of the community of the world meeting with our Lord so that we might be more effective in our work and witness every day. In one sense the church door ought always to be open, to invite in all who would to share with us as we meet with God and go out in the power of the Spirit.

Not every act of worship will be memorable. It would be foolish to imagine that we could live at that high level. Nonetheless we ought eagerly to anticipate meeting with the people of God as if it were a mountain top experience, like the disciples on the transfiguration mount seeing Jesus in a new way and sharing some of his secrets. When that happens worship has taken off and it is my testimony that this occurs often enough to make you eager for more. But it is vital to remember that the disciples had to leave the transfiguration mount. Peter was not allowed to erect his three tents so that they might all stay there for good. There was a world of need down in the valley, with a demon-possessed boy crying for help. We need our mountain tops in worship so that we might be the more effective in the valleys which await us outside the church door. Into those valleys we should go with new hope because we have gained a new confidence from our Lord himself.

6

Send Us Out

Healthy Christians at worship should always have half an
eye on the world outside and the other half on the world
inside. Far from the church at worship being an inward-
looking, cosy club, there we should be most conscious of
the outsider in the midst, the seeker and enquirer
hesitantly pushing open the door of the church of Christ.
In his famous chapter in 1 Corinthians chapter 14 on the
respective merits of speaking in tongues and prophecy,
one of Paul's great arguments is that the church at
worship should be particularly mindful of the one who is
from outside. Paul asked very pointedly how the outsider
can say 'Amen' to a prayer that he cannot understand. He
will call Christians mad if they speak in a language which
has no meaning to him, and yet he may be convicted of sin
and fall to the ground in worship when he hears a word
that is meaningful and relevantly brought home to him by
the Spirit.

If the church is going to be effective in its priority
ministry of evangelism we must be mindful of those
occasions when the outsider is actually inside. How
sensitive we must be that he is made to feel welcome and
that the services are not mumbo-jumbo. Paul cares that all

who come to church should be edified, and this applies to the one who will come with virtually no knowledge of the gospel. Christian services are not always to be kindergarten material; they must also provide for mature Christians who need to be built up even more. But certainly great care needs to be taken that the person on the edge of things is drawn in and not driven away. This calls for a careful understanding of how that person feels and a willingness to regulate our worship so that they can feel that they are wanted and that our ministry is relevant to them.

For those who love a challenge there is a great excitement in evangelism today. The gap between churchgoer and non-churchgoer has become infinitely wider with the decreasing knowledge of Scripture among most people. It is not uncommon today to welcome students to a church service and discover that they have never worshipped in a church in their lives before. There are advantages in this, in that fewer today are inoculated against the gospel by a dose of religion in their childhood. The message and the atmosphere of the church can come fresh and new to them.

We must be aware of the gulf that exists. In an odd way I was made aware of this when my verger had to rebuke a gentleman for smoking in the back pew of church, and his comment was that he did not see any no smoking notice around! This little incident highlights the foreign nature of the church to many people who occasionally visit us. The language we use in prayer books and hymn books and indeed in the jargon of Christian conversation is strange to newcomers. They do not see why they should sit quietly before the service – that is not how they behave when they go to a concert or a football match. They find it hard to understand a group who meet and yet do not seem to communicate with one another. There can be acute embarrassment when church people studiously ignore the newcomer. A sensitive outsider is also very aware of 'in' groups and 'in' language.

We must build many bridges into the church so that people are able to come (preferably already with friends) and are prepared for our church worship. But bridges are meant to get somewhere. Often the church has built bridges which nobody ever crosses. The church is wise to have in-roads into the community and to have community events within church buildings, but to be honest to its cause and its Master the church must be clear that she is not apologising about the gospel but is seeking to use the bridge to link the unbeliever with the Saviour.

There is a very obvious link between worship and evangelism. All true worship will send us out into the world with new vision and joy or new conviction. A Communion service, for example, often ends with a challenge to go in peace and serve the Lord. Worship is always open-ended. The sermon coming at the climax of worship should make the hearer eager to get out to obey the challenge. A subtle temptation of the devil is to encourage Christians to spend all their time together and imagine that the multiplicity of meetings is a measure of great holiness. We certainly do need to meet together and Christians should give a priority to their Sunday worship and mid-week gathering for prayer and study. But it is possible to be highly active in church affairs and completely ineffective in evangelistic enterprise. How often the sad lament has been heard when evangelism is announced that Christians do not have non-Christian friends to invite to hear the word. That is a desperate indictment.

If worship should send us out, there is nothing like

evangelism to send us back into the church! To be thrown in at the deep end witnessing for the Lord is to be made aware of how much we need constant renewal and strengthening. This will be particularly true for Christians who are witnessing and working in frontier situations. We are mostly aware these days of the need to commission people who go out in missionary service and to be involved prayerfully with them. Far less often do we recognise a similar need for those who are serving the Lord either in full-time Christian work or in a secular occupation in the tough areas of our own country. I believe that all churches should ask how much encouragement they are giving to those who do serve the Lord in these areas. We need to give such people more time to share with us their urgent needs. They should be able to feel that there is an ear which is open to their deep concerns and disappointments as well as their joys and successes. We should be providing the input which gives some inspiration for another week of giving out in often apparently unrewarding service to others. All this is built into the biblical idea of the body of Christ which must be a constant inspiration and challenge to us.

When the risen Lord appeared to the disciples in the upper room in John chapter 20 it was very important to them that he not only revealed himself and spoke of peace. He also gave them a new mission for life: 'as the Father has sent me even so I send you' (verse 21). To those who had failed Jesus so badly and who felt that there was nothing left that they could do, this commissioning was just as important as the comfort of the presence of the risen Lord. Jesus had come through shut doors which should have been open. It should never be the mark of the people of God when they meet together that they keep the world outside. The risen Lord was to break down those shut doors and at the Ascension would give the final great commission to his disciples, with the whole world as the sphere of evangelistic action. Any experience of Jesus should always culminate in a desire to share the truth with others.

The Old Testament has a slightly bizarre story of the lepers outside the walls of Samaria who were dying of starvation and then discovered that the enemy had left their camp. As they ate their fill they suddenly became conscience-stricken about the people inside Samaria who were dying when they could have lived. In the midst of the banquet they reminded each other, 'We're not doing right. This is a day of good news and we are keeping it to ourselves' (2 Kings 7:9, NIV). Christians who do not share in evangelism are guilty of silence. In a world where there is both great ignorance and great hunger for the truth of God we dare not be silent. Some may have a particular gift for evangelism. Scripture calls us all to be witnesses and to engage in the spreading of the good news.

There are very many different levels of evangelism and all of them matter. I have been privileged to be involved in many spheres of evangelism and sometimes think that that was why providentially I was given the name Philip! He sets a good example of evangelism in the Acts of the Apostles and I am proud to follow humbly in his footsteps. Evangelism has been defined as 'the presentation of the whole Christ, for the whole man, by the whole church, in the whole world'. By that very definition no Christian can be absolved from involvement. There cannot be effective evangelism without the whole church being committed to it. Tragically it has been seen as the interest of the elite. There can be no church without evangelism and therefore it is illogical for any Christian to opt out of the responsibility to take the good news into the world.

Whatever the methods, there must be a central act of proclamation. The whole Christ is to be proclaimed. This will inevitably mean some concentration of the message, as in the *kerygma* (the condensed essentials of the gospel) of the Acts of the Apostles. The early chapters of that book are well worth studying to see how Peter and the others concentrated the message on the person, the death, the resurrection and the coming again of Jesus, and all linked with the Pentecost experience of the Spririt. They and Paul after them always believed that the mind had to be convinced, and we often read of Paul in the synagogue arguing, setting scripture by scripture in order to convince the minds of his audience of the truths about Jesus. Some evangelism has taken on the nature of emotional manipulation rather than the conviction of the mind by the truth of Jesus. Inevitably, when the reality of our sinfulness and the love of our Saviour becomes real to us the emotions will be stirred, and we must take care not to be fearful of emotions.

We are called to proclaim the whole Christ. In different ages the church has been guilty of dismembering Jesus and producing a rather unbalanced gospel. With the proclamation of the gospel will go social implications. It is a message for the whole man, and that involves his physical and social condition as well as his eternal state. But we should certainly not err on the other side and be so concerned about social amelioration that we forget that ultimately man's eternal destiny affects all else.

Within this proclamation there will be those who have been given by the Spirit the particular gift to be evangelists. The story of the birth of the church in Samaria in Acts chapter 8 is very instructive. It all started with the gossiping of the gospel by those who were scattered through the persecution following the death of

Stephen, and then Philip the preacher came with a message that drew in the gospel net. In such a way the whole church today should be involved in the life-giving proclamation.

From the days of Pentecost there has been mass evangelism, and I have always found it difficult to understand those who object to it in principle, since there can be no greater evangelistic crusade than that in Jerusalem in which three thousand people were brought into the kingdom. With our modern technological achievements we may make Pentecost numerically pale by comparison. We must, while there is time, buy up this unique opportunity through the mass media. It was my remarkable privilege to chair Mission England-Sheffield meetings relayed by satellite to many parts of our country and beyond. Seeing the gospel preached in this kind of way simultaneously to many thousands of people made one appreciate the possibilities of evangelising the world in preparation for the Lord's return. It is a challenge to Christian giving and to our sense of priority and vision.

All too often the church fails by being neither small enough nor big enough. We often miss out on the unique opportunities of one-to-one conversations and sometimes we fail to think big enough in outreach ministry. There are limitations to mass evangelism, but my experience of chairing meetings at Bramall Lane, Sheffield United Football Ground, proved to me beyond measure the value of this kind of outreach. Apart from the thousands who were reached and the thousands who made profession, there is the great value of the whole church being united in preparation, in prayer and service. It would be foolish to deny that sometimes there are problems within that unity. Decisions have to be made as to how far it extends. Some Christians still remain very narrow in their view and would limit it unnecessarily. But obviously it matters that there should be a united belief in the gospel we preach and in the need for conversion. Within that context for Christians to get to know one another in service is the most wonderful kind of unifying force. I believe that even if not a soul had been reached during that outreach year something very significant would have happened in the Christian community through Christians praying and working together.

Trading on the personality is often condemned in Scripture and Christians need to be careful not to fall into the trap of a worldly personality cult. But equally there is something significant in the way in which the name of a person like Billy Graham will both attract people to the meetings and also interest the media. I believe the church is right to utilise this opportunity in order to reach people with the gospel. The apostle Paul was concerned to reach people by all means. It is heartening to know that with all his personality exposure Billy Graham down the years has always been studiously careful to direct people away from himself and to the churches. One of the acid tests of the integrity of a man's ministry is that he does not seek to build up a church around himself. With that proviso and also the utter faithfulness of Billy Graham to the biblical message, this kind of mass evangelism strengthens the arm of the churches and reaches people not normally touched by the ministry of the local Christian community.

On the other hand my constant cry during the very busy year of preparation for Mission England-Sheffield was that this was an event organised by the churches and feeding back into the churches. At no other level would I have been willing to give up so much of my ministerial time to the support and administration of this venture. Where the local church was alive, here was an unequalled opportunity to train our members in the work of evangelism and counselling. There were jobs for everyone, including the very young Christians not yet ready for tasks demanding spiritual maturity. They could be involved in the choir or as stewards or in other practical jobs that brought them very close to the heart of the gospel ministry, and it was exciting to see that people who had been involved at this level were as deeply moved by the sight of people being won for Christ as those who were more in the centre of things.

All who responded went back to the local church, and as a result of the very careful follow-up procedure the nurture groups set up in many local churches were as significant as the main meetings themselves. In this way mass evangelism is no contradiction of the work of the local church. It was a very interesting experience to be both chairman of the large venture and a vicar of a parish church receiving those who went forward. There is no doubt at all that the many smaller groups within the life of our church have been enhanced by this whole evangelistic enterprise and the ripples flowing from it have continued long after the main meetings ended. In assessing the value of Mission England-Sheffield it is not enough to look at the statistics of those who went forward and their continued commitment. It is also important to see how many more have been coming into the orbit of the church and ultimately to Christ because of those who themselves went forward at the meetings or simply through the renewed confidence in the gospel which was engendered in Christians by the enterprise.

However, even a large venture like this falls very far short of the presentation of the whole Christ in the whole world. Overseas missionary work is vital, but we are also aware that whole tracts of our own cities are left untouched by this kind of evangelism. No evangelistic effort will reach all people and it is folly to refuse support because of the shortcomings of any venture. Yet the Christian church must consider very carefully how to reach the untouched areas and to break down the cultural barriers which afflict all kinds of mass evangelism. I believe that because it is a unique opportunity as a focal point for prayer and action an event like a Billy Graham mission must be seized whenever the opportunity comes, and we need to pray that there will be more men of the calibre of Billy Graham, preferably from the British Isles, who will be able to cope with this kind of ministry. There should be endlessly increasing opportunities to use the mass media in evangelism, and it would be tragic if we failed to capitalise on this because there seemed to be nobody raised up for the purpose. Here is a challenge to our prayer and vision.

But alongside this sort of very occasional united effort there is the ongoing work of the local church, and here the cause of evangelism is ultimately lost or won. It is my increasing conviction that the best centre for effective evangelism is the local church. I have been privileged to lead over thirty parish missions in different parts of the country, some in four of the largest Church of Ireland parishes in Northern Ireland. It all started when as a curate I assisted the Bishop of Liverpool in his town mission to Widnes. As a very raw recruit I found the challenge somewhat intimidating, but the Lord was good and there was some fruit from that mission seen in the small daughter church which was my particular sphere of service. Over the years things have changed. I would now take far more meetings in the smaller home group setting rather than in the church building. There are still exceptions to this in churches which are already well organised and well attended. Inevitably the numbers reached are more limited where the home group is the centre, almost without exception I believe the percentage of non-Christians hearing the gospel is higher when we meet in an informal way in homes.

This highlights the effectiveness of a special evangelistic thrust within the local church. The setting is natural. The neighbour is invited quite normally by a friend, and although the gospel message is clearly presented, there is a low-key atmosphere. It is my belief that where people are more relaxed and feel less threatened they are more likely to respond to the good news. Even if the meetings are held in the local church building, it has the advantage of being in the familiar neighbourhood of the person being reached. Also, immediate and unforced follow-up procedures are much easier in a local setting.

For the past decade I have been sharing evangelistic enterprise with members of my own congregation, and this has had very many advantages. In a slightly selfish way it means I, away from my own parish, am still doing the work of a parish minister, leading my own people in a shared enterprise. We benefit as much as the people we reach. But even more than this, the testimony of people from different walks of life undergirds the gospel message and ministry. People relate very quickly to those who are speaking, and especially where we do not choose 'experts' who are good at giving testimonies or who have a very exciting testimony to thrill the audience. The people who go with me normally are members of one of our home groups, and often the rather hesitant testimony of someone doing it for the first time has a greater power, simply because it is clearly taking much out of the person concerned. I believe that the word of testimony is a very sensitive weapon. It can so easily give the impression of egocentricity, that the person is glorifying himself. There is a place for the exciting conversion story, but often this is less effective because it clearly does not relate to most of the people who listen.

Within the context of an intimate group in the home, with the possibility of conversational come-back afterwards, I have found that the combination of a simple gospel message with an illustration from daily life by testimony or by song has a great power. Normally we feed into a closing service at the end of the week where responses can be open, but again in a low-key manner. I believe it to be vital to demonstrate that a response to Christ is not just that of going forward at a meeting, but it is a commitment for life and will affect the whole of daily living. In some ways I play down the actual commitment moment because I have seen so many people who have responded in an emotional atmosphere but have hardly moved on from that point. Commitment will involve the emotions but it is the will which counts, and certainly the person responding should be made aware that it has to do with ordinary life and not just with religious activity.

I have not only shared in parish missions in many places and with many different backgrounds – inner city and mining communities as well as suburban and rural parishes – but I have also been at the receiving end of parish missions in my own churches, and so I know the value of 'home-grown' evangelism. In fact I believe that I have been able to present myself as not primarily an evangelist but as a parish minister. The Lord does call some into full-time evangelism, and praise God for them. But I believe many more local ministers could be effective in helping in outreach ventures in other churches, not least because they know from experience how an evanglistic crusade can effect a local church. It has been commented that some missioners leave such a mess behind that the minister probably wishes that he had never set out on the evangelistic venture. A good evangelist always remembers that it is the local Christians who will face the music when he is gone.

In seeing the Lord at work in parish missions I have been very conscious of the value within the local community of Christians meeting to pray, hence the tremendous blessing of the prayer triplet scheme which burst upon us in Mission England. I would personally testify to the value of week-by-week meeting with two members of my own congregation to pray in this way. But preparation involves more than prayer, and the imminence of a parish or local church mission will inevitably encourage more systematic door-to-door visitation in the neighbourhood. On the whole this kind of visitation tends to be decried today as somewhat unproductive. I happen to believe that there are plenty of surprises when we dare to launch out in this way, and often we rationalise our cowardice by concentrating our contacts with those who are already apparently half way to the kingdom. In virtually every mission I have taken there have been some people coming to faith contacted through this means who might otherwise never have been in touch with the life of the church. It is a daunting exercise but I believe it pays dividends, not just in the immediate contacts made but in the awareness it fosters that the church means business and the encouragement it gives to Christians to get their teeth into some face-to-face contact with the non-Christians around them. Also, visitation is much more likely to be effective if those visiting are known to be people living in the same area.

While it is easy for Christians to compartmentalise their lives and keep their Christian fellowship in a different compartment from their neighbourhood or friends at work, the local church and the parish mission affords the most obvious opportunity to break down the wall between those compartments. We are constantly challenged to be living for Christ in our daily work and relationships, and it ought therefore to be comparatively easy to seek to introduce our friends in the world to our Saviour when we have established a relationship of trust and love. It may not be natural to wait for some special event in the church to become vocal, but it does provide an unusual opening and my experience has been that some of the converts who best stood the test of time have come through that kind of relationship coming to a head at a time of mission.

It is only fair to point out that also here are the greatest hurts, when friendships built up over a period do not bear fruit, and sometimes a relationship can be soured because of a friend's reluctance to respond to our invitation to the gospel. This is the inevitable double edge of Christian witness. The danger in the local church or the university or college having a mission every three or four years is that there can be too great a dependence upon the occasional event and then a very complacent lethargy sets in during the intervening period. But when the Spirit really begins to move, then somehow the zeal for evangelism will spill over and the occasional will become the normal.

My contention that local evangelism is always the most effective is largely because the immediate follow-up is not engineered but is already there. On the assumption that the church is doing its job throughout the year, there will be groups of one kind or another ready to receive those who respond during the preaching of the gospel. The groups will be sufficiently established for them to be warm and loving, but open enough to receive new people. It may be wise to have nurture groups to deal with the immediate follow-up material, but is even more vital to know how to stop them than to know how to begin them. There are few thing worse than a nurture group which continues ad nauseam. This happens often because other groups either do not exist or have ceased to be outward-looking in love.

Local church evangelism makes churchgoing the easier in that already there are friends and familiar faces within that strange institution entered rather cautiously by the newly committed. Also, with evangelism on the local church scale the difference between the great evangelistic event and the ordinary Sunday is not too marked. However we may play it down, it must seem strange for the person who responds with the thousands in some football stadium to realise that the sincere but often fairly amateur worship on Sunday with thirty or forty people around is the same thing. There is not the same gap when the gospel is preached within the context of the local community and fellowship. If that local church is at all alive, then evangelism will not be a plan for the special event but the day-to-day normality of life.

Evangelism should be a normal activity within worship. This does not mean that every sermon should be 'evangelistic' as such, but there is no real line of demarcation between teaching and evangelism. Faithful exposition of Scripture will inevitably merge the two, and it is a commonplace in a church where the Bible is expounded that Christians are taught and edified at the same time as non-Christians are challenged to commitment. It is therefore idle to differentiate too closely between an ordinary act of worship and an evangelistic service. Oddly enough, the outsider may be less inclined to come to a guest service, knowing what might befall him, than he is to come to an ordinary act of worship.

With the subtlety of a serpent we sometimes should strike when he is not ready! On the other hand, there is naturally a lot to be said for focusing interest in particular services, and I have for many years used the concept of a guest service with some degree of blessing attached to it. For example, young people do like to work towards a special service in which they take part, and well prepared, this can be effective not only for young people and their interested parents but across the whole spectrum of the church.

The same can be true of a student service or a marriage reunion service or one for those who have had children baptised or dedicated. It certainly means that the special occasion which naturally draws the outsider should be well utilised. Too often we cater for people's sentimentality at Christmas, instead of using the moment to drive home the great evangel that is at the heart of the Christmas message. It is quite inexcusable to allow that momentous hour to degenerate into a rather childish, sickly occasion. On the other hand it is sad when rigorists miss the opportunity because they fear tradition too much. A little wisdom can blend tradition and the gospel beautifully. A similar thing could be said for Mothering Sunday, which needs to be rescued from its emptiness, and even Remembrance Day, with its many problems, has its own significance.

Within this context the commitment made by the individual is very often a very gradual matter and I increasingly believe it to be helpful not to insist on some commitment at that point in time, although that can be valuable for some. I have found so many people who later will testify to what has been happening over a period of time. Paul's comment in Romans 10:9 still stands, that there must be confession with the lips as well as belief in the heart. But that confession could well come long after the Rubicon has been crossed. Many of the people who have come to faith in my ministry have never expressed it at a particular point but have looked back and then have made their confession which has stood the test of time.

In the evangelism centred on the normal life of the church the different groups have their own place. Children's work is basically teaching, caring and nurturing, but there are obvious opportunities for encouraging children to come to a place of commitment, with the proviso that it is seen as a children's act of commitment. We should not seek to press upon them the mature response of an adult. Alongside the regular teaching of the Sunday groups there are countless opportunities these days of evangelistic ventures at holiday time, when children are only too eager to find an opportunity of relief from the boredom of long holidays.

With teenagers this is even more significant and it would be interesting to know how many young people, like myself, come to Christ through camps and houseparties. The local church should be able in some measure to put its resources in ventures which concentrate on outreach to young people. These are demanding, and the church must be ready to pay the price both in time, manpower and money. My own church may have been ususual in its ability to have a full-time youth worker for a number of years, but I have no doubt that the expenditure has paid rich dividends beyond our reckoning. Teenagers are so often won to Christ by the fact that their peers witness to them in an attractive way, and the Christian young person, often under pressure these days, needs to have help and encouragement from good leadership. It also makes evangelism so much easier if there is a youth club which is well run and attractive. In due course the teenager on the frontier can be drawn into the church family because of the attractiveness of a fairly secular youth club run within a Christian church. Evangelism in that context is a natural on-going thing.

I have a deep concern for evangelism amongst men, with the awareness that in mass evangelism adult men are very low in the statistical list. I have hardly ever seen any kind of mass evangelism where this is not the case. This is reflected in the life of the church, and of course we begin a vicious circle at this point. All too often the women are the ones who use the evangelistic opportunity and it is the women who are won for Christ – at which we rejoice, of course. But where there is not a strong male element the church will inevitably be the weaker. Men's suppers and men's breakfasts are opportunities where men will naturally gather together. We need to look at the worship of the church to make sure that it does not seem effeminate to the average male. There is a kind of manly evangelism which enables non-Christian men with integrity to face up to the challenge of Christ. I believe that this is an area where we need to be bold, and it deserves more priority than it usually gets.

But of course, evangelism among women is vital, and there has been an upsurge through women's lunches and suppers of that kind of ministry in a natural context. It needs to be well done, comparing well with the world in its standards and yet infinitely better in its care and love. The world can be a very hard place, and many a person is open to the gospel because he or she has been offered very obvious friendship and an open ear. The local playgroup in the church gives an opening to young mothers. Many women at that age are lonely and facing a new moment in their lives, and are therefore vulnerable to the gospel. To reach them at that time is not just to be subtle; it is to meet a felt need, and not one that we have suggested.

Evangelism among older people is an area where we need sensitivity, but most churches can very easily run senior citizens groups for meals and fellowship. We need not apologise for introducing the gospel at this point, and indeed I believe we have a responsibility to do so. How easy it is to be content to be the sort of church which provides for the communal needs of people and never mentions their eternal needs. I believe that to be treacherous, and even if a gospel context earns the church a little unpopularity because we are not just being a social agency, the price is worth paying. Naturally, to speak of eternal issues to folk for whom death is becoming an imminent reality calls for much grace. But this is not an excuse for keeping our mouths shut.

For most churches the links through baptism or dedication, weddings or funerals are not to be missed. The regular visitation from Christians to people's homes in connection with these and other events provides another opening. It is good for the local church to keep people constantly mindful that there is a church around the corner, without becoming oppressively persistent. We may be challenged by the dedication of Jehovah's Witnesses; we need to be careful not to be quite as rudely insistent as they sometimes are.

All this probably means that the church should dare to publicise well and to think seriously about the money we spend at that level. If such publicity is attractive and clearly modern, it gives an image of the church which is likely to attract. It may be a long time before the person who reads a parish magazine or an invitation to a meeting actually dares to step inside the church building. But an impact has been made. Then it matters that alongside the attractive image the reality of the church inside matches. Sometimes posters outside a church proclaim its welcome and love and the atmosphere inside preaches the opposite.

At the end of the day all evangelism hinges on the one-by-one encounter. However vast the audience in which someone hears the gospel, it is almost always proclaimed through the lips of one person, and the counselling will also be effectively done by one. I confess that I personally am much happier in the context of one with many, and therefore I always have enormous admiration for those who effectively engage in this intimate ministry of speaking of the Lord to another. There are snares, and some in seeking to speak to others at every given opportunity can become insensitive. Normally rudeness does not commend the gospel. Most Christians, however, are more in danger of undue timidity. Still in my congregations I have known a number of people who, because of very special gifts in this direction, have hovered on the verge of being rude and yet have been much used by the Lord. Perhaps it was rude of Philip to jump on the chariot carrying the Ethiopian chancellor back home. God honoured that rudeness. Indeed, in that particular section of Acts it almost seems that the potential converts were more ready to listen than the committed Christians to speak. Peter was very reluctant to go to Cornelius and Ananias argued the toss with the Almighty before he went to welcome Saul. Only Philip was raring to go! My experience has been that this is still often true. We are so anxious not to upset that very often we miss golden opportunities.

In all this the Lord uses human personality. A very apt definition of preaching has been 'truth mediated through personality'. It applies equally to the word of testimony from the lips of the ordinary Christian. Sometimes the young Christian has a degree of enthusiasm that some more mature people have sadly lost. Again it has been said that evangelism is 'one beggar telling another beggar where to find bread'. We have sometimes become so used to the meal that we have forgotten what it was like when we were so hungry. Yet with all this personal initiative, there is a real place for training in evangelism, if only to help people to avoid pitfalls. I have seen role-plays demonstrating how not to do it which have been too near to the mark to be really funny.

But training must always leave much to the individual. In my earnest cricketing days I discovered that all the careful coaching by the experts was fairly useless if there was not the spark of personal ability and sadly, real ability was often coached to death and the end result was something rather ordinary. It is possible to train people into a mould, and that would be tragic. All training should lead to practice and the practice of evangelism is best served not so much by dropping a whole load of Christians into the marketplace and telling them to get on with it, but asking Christians within the normal friend-ship contexts to practise what they have learned in their training sessions. The Lord may sometimes use the very unusual, out-of-the-blue contact to lead someone to Christ, but we must not expect this to be the norm.

A church which is spiritually alive should always be expecting people to be converted. Without foolish counting of heads, we should look for the Lord to be adding daily to the church those who are being saved. There ought to be constant opportunities for such people to be openly welcomed into the church, but often our Confirmation preparation or church membership classes have become rather stylised and unduly formal. With this welcoming there should be many opportunities for young Christians to speak of their faith, bearing in mind the warning of the Apostle Paul not to exalt a young Christian to a position of leadership too early. It is vital that a change in life should be clearly demonstrated. There have been too many casualties as a result of unwise parading of the convert in public. The greatest witness of the new Christian is to his or her non-Christian friends. Sometimes these begin to fade away despite the best intention in the world when the new Christian finds his new way of life. Levi was very wise to have his dinner party with his old friends fairly quickly, so they could meet the new friend Jesus. Often the young Christian can reach people who have gone out of the orbit of the long-established Christian community.

All this will be happening within the context of a church learning and obeying the word of the Lord. In the early church this was apparently the pattern, and in the story of the rise of the church in Antioch, after the first wave of conversions there was a year of teaching, and the record tells us that more people were added to the Lord. A church which has come alive through evangelism needs to be well taught; a church that is being taught will have a new desire to reach more for Christ, and so life multiplies.

7

The Ministry of the Word

————————— 🍃 —————————

Our Lord himself is the illustration of the greatest evangelist at work, and to see him in action is the best training ground you will ever find. It is an excellent exercise to watch him dealing with people in the gospel record and to see the kind of sensitivity which he had and his great blend of grace and truth. Equally, he remains the greatest example of the teacher at work, and we could never do better than to study his teaching ministry when we consider that aspect of the church's work today.

In the New Testament evangelism and teaching always go hand in hand. When he sent out the disciples into the world in his great commission at the end of Matthew's gospel, Jesus urges them to go and make disciples and to teach (Mt. 28:19-20). It is often difficult to differentiate between these two exercises, for many people have come to new life through the teaching ministry of the church. When the apostle Paul preached the good news he would regularly debate, dialogue or even argue with the religious people of his day. Although we live in a very different society with much less open discussion of God and Scripture, it is still vital that the mind should be reached in proclaiming Christ. Paul says something very significant in Romans

6:17 when he is discussing what happens at the point of conversion. He reminds us that all parts of the personality were involved in the conversion experience. He speaks of becoming obedient, which refers to the will; to the standard of teaching which refers to the mind; and in the phrase 'from the heart' he refers to the emotions. All evangelism must appeal to all three. There is a kind of decisionism practised today which challenges the will without much content, and there is also a great deal of emotionalism, which can create a response which is very superficial. Equally there can be a very cerebral presentation of the gospel which never gets beyond the intellect. The whole person must be involved.

If that is true at the beginning of the Christian experience, it is equally true in the continuance. Very often in his letters Paul is adamant about the importance of the edification and up-building of the church. This stands out most of all in 1 Corinthians chapters 12 and 14, where he is discussing the place of the gifts of the Spirit and is at great pains to emphasise that the use of the gifts should be for edification and up-building. This is why he discourages excessive enthusiasm for the gift of tongues in public worship and encourages the gift of prophecy. Argument will rage about the exact meaning of prophecy in Paul's writings and its relationship with all that happens in the church today. I believe it to be more than preaching, but no preaching worthy of the name should be less than prophetic. It is possible to expound scripture without any prophetic word for today and that ultimately is not preaching, however good the exegesis may be. We are not out to create learned theologians in our preaching but born-again and mature Christians. There is a place for a more spontaneous word from the Lord which must not be discredited, although it should always be judged by

Scripture (1 Cor. 14:29). The aim of the prophetic word must always be to build people up into maturity.

I recollect being suddenly challenged by a young student some years ago as to what was the aim of my ministry. Sometimes that slightly rude questioning is good for the health of the minister. After a little thought I went back to Paul's great affirmation in Colossians 1:28. My main aim would be 'to present every man mature in Christ'. This will mean a great stress not only on the milk of the word for the young Christian but also the meat for the health of the growing Christian. Every church should have some kind of nurture group for those who are young in faith, but it will fail if its regular teaching ministry remains at the a-b-c level (see Heb. 6:1).

The church's teaching programme is much more than a pulpit ministry. That in itself must never be neglected, however. He will find a good biblical precedent in Nehemiah chapter 8, and I believe there is a place for an authoritative proclamation. But much teaching will take place at other levels.

It means that those who teach children themselves should be well instructed. It is nothing less than tragic when we consider how lightly we have treated this vital area of our ministry. In the days when Sunday School was accepted for all children, so often the end product was utterly ill-informed young people who were delighted when they could throw off the shackles of Sunday School. Of course, there were glorious exceptions, and some of us rejoice that we were well taught in those days. With fewer numbers now in our Sunday School we have less excuse, and yet all too often it is the Cinderella of the church's life and we assume that anyone can look after the children. It is almost as bad with young people, and often it is assumed that children and young people simply want to be entertained or want to have baby stuff. With minds that are formative and eagerly learning in every realm, we should set our sights high. I believe it to be a vital maxim that we never teach a child anything that he or she must unlearn when they grow up. In an odd kind of way I have always believed that to bring up children on the myth of Father Christmas is to put them in danger of equating Jesus with that figure, whom the adult rejects as a childish myth. In Christian things a child can learn profound truths at his or her own level, and often have a deeper faith than many a questioning adult.

The groups within the church ought not to be just occasions for fellowship and sharing but also places of learning. We have gone through an orgy of the sharing kind of meeting, where all the attention is focused on us and our problems and experiences. There is a place for this kind of openness in order that we may be helped and that people might pray for us, but it becomes very unhealthy as the norm of group work. Rather, it is as we learn together that we deepen and open ourselves more to the Lord and his truths and to one another.

Every minister or Christian leader should make a priority of planning the preaching and teaching in the Sunday worship. I have always made it a priority at summer holiday time to look ahead to the whole year and to seek to find a kind of pattern of teaching which will be balanced. I believe that if the preacher is planning and is excited about the truth, he will probably carry the congregation with him. If he seems to be always rushing at the last minute with some thought for the day he will produce fairly thin and immature Christians.

Alongside the ministry of the local church there is a place for a wider teaching ministry, and I personally believe that the Keswick Convention has had a remarkable history at this level and still has much to teach those younger conventions and gatherings which now abound throughout the country. The teaching of the Keswick Convention has been primarily focused on personal, practical and Scriptural holiness and has developed a scheme of teaching which has helped in this respect. Every scheme can become a tyrannical master and there is no sacred cow about the Keswick pattern, nor is there really any Keswick teaching. It is biblical teaching, but with this particular emphasis. We look together over the weekend at the glory of God and then focus on sin in the life of the believer on Monday. Then on Tuesday we consider the wonder of our Lord's atoning sacrifice and what it means for a life of victory. On Wednesday we consider the lordship of Christ and its implications. Thursday is the day when we expound the ministry of the Spirit in the life of the believer and all that this means in a life of holiness. Finally on Friday we see some of the implications of Spirit-filled living as we look out to the world and its need.

There was a time when the Keswick Convention made a great play on sanctification as a crisis experience, but this is to look very much at the Keswick of the past, and all the preachers at Keswick in this day and age would reject the idea of a second blessing experience as much as they would be critical of the thought that the baptism in the Spirit is a necessary second experience for the believer. 1 Corinthians 12:13 makes it very clear that the baptism in the Spirit is that unique moment for every Christian when he or she is regenerated in the Spirit. The biblical teaching on holiness calls for obedience and a progressive experience of the Spirit in life. But of course, in that progressive experience there are constant challenges and the value of a convention ministry like Keswick is to bring people together in one great concourse under the authority of Scripture expounded in a truly prophetic manner.

Not always do we at Keswick live up to the expectations of those who gather. Often people come in vain, and certainly this century-old Convention cannot rest on its laurels. Many of us involved in the Convention are eagerly seeking to make it more attractive to a younger generation, without in any way changing the emphasis of its message. There are groups of people meeting together who would lay much more emphasis on experience and worship, and these will have their place. Keswick stands or falls by the quality of the exposition of God's word, although in these days we need to recognise that people often listen better when there is more active congregational participation, and we have even introduced seminars where people can more actively contribute in the teaching process.

My twenty years of involvement with Keswick have been an enriching experience for me and I still believe that there is an urgent need for this Convention and others like it throughout the country and the world which will encourage people to get to grips with God's word and with a particular concern for a life of holiness. Ultimately that is God's concern for me – that I should live a life which is pleasing to him and glorifies Jesus.

I have never forgotten that at my ordination, as I mentioned before, the symbol of my new ministry was the Bible handed to me as a mark of the authority under which I was to work. At the Reformation this was one of the great revolutions. No more did the priest receive a chalice as a symbol of his ministry, but rather the Scriptures, and that revolution took the church back to the biblical perspective. But this can be an idle piece of ceremony unless all who minister are constantly aware that they are under the word of God. It is a frightening thing to prepare messages week by week and to recognise that it is impossible to preach with integrity until the preacher has been subject to the truth himself. I always find Jeremiah a great comfort in that he, in spite of his occasional rebellion, trembled at the word and at the same time had that fire in his belly which could not be contained.

It is a privilege to counsel would-be ministers thinking in terms of ordination, and I always enquire on two levels as to their sense of passion. In the first place I seek to discover whether there is a passion for the word of God. The potential preacher may have had little scope for preaching, but at least there ought to be a sense of deep desire to communicate that word to others. Equally I enquire about a passion for souls. The phrase may be somewhat archaic but the reality should always be fresh. A minister must love people as well as love the word. It is very possible for someone to enjoy the word of God but to be utterly aloof, and it is equally possible for people to be caring and loving but have no word from the Lord. Neither of these would make true ministers of the gospel. In our age we should look not for more ministers but for those who have this double passion. We need not have too many of such people to transform things radically.

There is a certain danger in being in a position of proclaiming the truth with dogmatic assurance. Normally the preacher is not in a position to be questioned, and indeed it is arguable that the word of God is not to be discussed but obeyed. Therefore the preacher must have a stern self-discipline. The pulpit is not the place to throw out ideas and theories or to speak dogmatically on issues on which the Bible does not speak clearly. Then the congregation will rightly become restive, since they can disagree with an equal Christian mind and have no place to argue the toss. Of course, there is a place for seminars and discussions on controversial issues. But the teaching ministry of the word of God has such an authority that the preacher himself must have already responded to the word. He would be wise to speak much more in the first person than the second person when preaching. Because there is great power in the proclamation, there is great need for responsible use of it. I suppose that one of the great safeguards is a knowledge of people and a love for them. The sermon does not stand in isolation but it is all part and parcel of a pastoral ministry.

But teaching does not begin and end in the pulpit. There is a great principle in the New Testament of instructing others who will continue the good work. So our Lord spent a great deal of his precious time instructing rather reluctant disciples in the truth so that they might be equipped to continue the work when he had gone. 2 Timothy 2:2 expresses a very great principle of action: 'what you have heard from me before many witnesses entrust to faithful men who will be able to teach others also'. You see the sequence? Paul – Timothy – faithful men – others also. In this kind of way the work is multiplied, and it could well be the failure of the church in the days when people did listen to sermons and preachers did preach with conviction that there was not the training of others to communicate the message themselves. That principle should be written deep in the strategies of every local church.

Much teaching of this kind will be very personal and I believe we need to give more time to the small group in the ministry of teaching. Also one-to-one ministry and counselling should always have a high place in the work of the church, but we must beware of the danger of making a god of counselling. I believe that I am sometimes deemed heretical in my view that the success of a sermon is not measured by how many people stay to be counselled but how few. Very often if the word has been preached clearly and gone home effectively it is a matter between the individual and the Lord. All is clear and the person is able to sort it out himself or herself. Of course, this is over-simplistic, and there will always be people with issues that need to be talked over with a mature Christian friend. In an age when ministering to one another has become quite a common thing after a church service there is much to commend and much to criticize. It is not always wise to unburden yourself to an unknown person who happens to be sitting next to you, and it is always tempting for the person who is eager to counsel to find problems where they do not exist or to escalate them into something grandiose when often it is quite a simple matter. How many people have discovered demons where no demon has ever been? My experience at the Keswick Convention is that often many people who stay for counselling are there because they are bewildered, not because we have brought home the challenge of the gospel in the power of the Spirit. Some of the most effective meetings have been followed by a quiet going home, to put right what God has clearly said to us.

In Scripture there is always a balance between the word and the Spirit. Right from Genesis chapter 1 they work hand in hand, as 'God said...' and 'the Spirit of God was moving on the face of the waters'. On the day of Pentecost the Spirit came, the crowds were drawn by the praising of God in tongues, and then Peter preached. After the preaching thousands were converted and the Spirit moved afresh. In the home of Cornelius Peter was still in the middle of expounding the truth when the Spirit fell upon

Cornelius and the household, and baptism had to follow. We are meant to be true to the word, and then the Spirit will drive home its message and make it real in the lives of individuals. It is not unlike the moment in the Old Testament when Elijah was contesting with the false prophets. After he had made all the preparation that was necessary and had prayed, then the fire fell. Only God can bring the fire; only we can do the preparation. An ill-prepared sermon should not expect the fire to fall, but also a sermon studiously prepared without prayer may be beautiful and eloquent, but quite dead.

Where God has joined together, sadly men have often put asunder. Some of us major on the word and are very fearful of the Spirit. We are true to Scripture but expect nothing to happen. It is possible to have good doctrine but no life. Also, many churches today major on the Spirit but with little exposition of the truth of Scripture. I believe this to be a very dangerous condition in the church. There is a heart-cry for teaching, and because there has been a resurgence of interest in and life through the Spirit the devil has found his niche by encouraging Christians to play down the need for doctrine and teaching. Is it not enough that we are united in the Spirit? Does truth matter any more, it is asked. A very dangerous maxim has been coined which goes something like this: 'Love unites, doctrine divides'. There may be truth in this from time to time, but to dissociate love and doctrine is a dangerous step. Word and Spirit must go together.

All this is the challenge to the local church and it is also a challenge to a movement like the Keswick Convention, which God has seen fit to honour over this past century. We are wise to warn people of the dangers of false teaching on the work of the Spirit. We are much wiser to concentrate on preaching a biblical doctrine of the Spirit, with special reference to his work in creating a life of holiness and Christ-likeness in the believer. When we preach in that kind of way we may expect God to be at work.

There is no monopoly of the Spirit's work, and some Christians, somewhat fearful of the excesses of the charismatic movement, have almost become guilty of explaining everything away and not expecting the Spirit to move in any evident manner. When there is healthy teaching and an expectation of the Spirit working within that context I believe we shall then have mature Christians, not children who are tossed to and fro with every latest religious fad and ready and ripe for the latest religious con trick. Children are characterised by not concentrating on anything for too long. Immature Christians are just the same.

But mature Christians should not be dull Christians. It is foolish to try to be like Peter Pan and not grow up beyond an infantile Christian experience. But it is a sign that things have gone stale if we grow prematurely old in our faith. When the Spirit is at work we are being constantly renewed and spiritually getting younger every day. That brand of Christianity is needed desperately and, I believe, much depends upon the quality of the minister who needs to be very mature and yet – by the grace of God – vigorous, alive, adaptable and ready for anything.

8

The Minister of the Word

In our society pressure is the name of the game. We are
constantly complaining of it and there is no doubt that our
particular age has produced a level of pressure upon the
individual and society which sometimes becomes
unbearable. Christians are not immune to this, nor is it
just a product of our twentieth century. The Greek word
for pressure comes often in the New Testament as in the
promise of our Lord in John 16:33 that in the world we
would have tribulation, which means pressure. The
apostle Paul, when he wants to boast of his achievements
as an apostle in order to off-set the arrogance of the false
apostles, will point not so much to his successes as to the
things he suffered and the cost he paid in Christian
service. Very often his opponents were much more ready
to boast of visions and status. To Paul the mark of belonging to Christ and being chosen for his service was seen in
hardship and pressurised living. A glance at his comments
in 2 Corinthians chapters 6 and 11 makes challenging
reading. Our Lord had clearly promised this experience
for the servant who followed his master when he prepared
the disciples for the battle in the upper room.

We are therefore not surprised that when Paul wants to

encourage young Timothy about the work of the ministry he uses analogies which are demanding ones. In 2 Timothy chapter 2 he likens the Christian ministry to the soldier and his dedication, to the athlete and his discipline, to the farmer and his sacrificial hard work. In all these areas of life conflict rather than comfort is the order of the day. The battle is on and we in the Christian ministry can particularly expect to have to wrestle with spiritual forces. Always the victory is sure, but there is no short cut to the enjoyment of that victory. The apostle Paul almost seemed to relish the thought of the fight, and any Christian ministry which goes soft on this point is bound to be sadly ineffective.

Part of that conflict lies in the sheer pace of church life today. It is inevitable that the church, competing in the right sense with the world around it, dare not live in a backwater and must keep up with the world. That pace will have its demands upon those who are called to leadership within the church. At the same time there are many aids to assist us in our work and ministry. It should be possible therefore for the minister to be released from many of the chores of a past age and be better able to give himself to the real work of the ministry. Just as in Acts help was called in to enable the apostles to concentrate on the ministry of the word and prayer, so today there are technological and mechanical aids to relieve the minister of certain aspects of work so that he might be more free for the priority ministry. Sadly it is easy to become obsessed with the aids and to allow whole chunks of time to be swallowed up in caring for the machine that is meant to release us for the work which we still too often neglect.

Tension also comes into the life of the minister because of the expectations of Christian people within the congregation or non-Christian people with whom we are in

114

contact. Alongside this there seems to be a sad uncertainty about the place of the ordained or full-time minister. Because the laity has become more mobilised there is the danger of one set apart for full-time ministry feeling unwanted and unnecessary. The day of the one man band has fortunately gone, and none too soon, although some still hanker after that anachronism. But there is still the reality of much loneliness in the ministry, and with it dangerous comparisons with those in the secular world who are the contemporaries of the full-time Christian worker. It is a day of crisis for the ministry.

Yet I want to use these pages as an opportunity to return thanks to God for thirty years of very happy and fulfilling ministry. I would be the first to acknowledge that I have been privileged to minister in favoured territory and I would not be critical of those for whom the ministry has often been a burden and a disappointment. But I can only testify to the fulfilment and joy in that ministry, not least because of its demands upon time and energy. The full-time Christian work more than any other vocation becomes all too consuming in the life of the minister and therefore it helps greatly when the minister's wife or husband is fully involved in the work with him or her. That partnership makes all the difference. But even so the Psalmist's comment is still very relevant: 'they who sow in tears shall reap in joy' (Ps. 126:5). The joy springs out of the tears, as in our Lord's analogy (Jn. 16:20-22) of the pain and joy of childbirth.

It is good in a day of crisis for the ministry to look afresh at our roots. On the other hand it is difficult to find in the New Testament parallels for much of the church leadership of our day. Certainly the New Testament seems more concerned with function than status and looks much more at the gifts which God gives than the positions which men hold. It is folly to assume that there is any one pattern of ministry in the New Testament. But there is clear precedent for a full-time or stipendiary ministry. Paul argues very eloquently in 1 Corinthians chapter 9 for his right to be paid in the ministry, a right which he will forego often in order not to be misunderstood. But he sees it as the norm that there should be a full-time paid ministry. He also makes much of a Christian being released from the normal cares of life so that he might be fully committed to his work, and certainly in 1 Corinthians chapter 7 he seems to suggest that for some people a celibate ministry enables them to be utterly devoted to the work. A happily married man in the ministry might equally argue that in most areas of ministry marriage to a partner fully committed to the Lord is a deeper act of release, so that the minister might be fully given to the Lord's service.

A ministry of preaching and teaching will demand much time in preparation, not only in the studying of the Scriptures themselves but also in reading and meditation about the relevance of the Scriptures to the world of today. The preacher is a bridge builder with firm foundations both in the world to which he ministers and the word from which he ministers. However gifted a preacher may be, the moment he ceases to give time to study, that moment he begins to become stale and very quickly this is apparent in his preaching. Pastoral care in its unhurried form also takes time, and there is no substitute for that unhurried ministry. There is a place for ministry at the end of a church service, but often that is superficial if not effectively followed up by visitation or regular counselling. So the minister needs to have time. But he must also be a disciplined person. There is a tremendous challenge in a life without specific hours of work.

Christian ministers err on both sides. Some work too hard and become proud of it. Others frankly live at a very easy pace. To be unaccountable to any human employer and to be privileged to run one's own time schedule calls for the truest discipline in the presence of the Lord.

Full-time ministry in our day has proliferated in a very exciting manner. More people are called into specialist roles and the church does need to have vision wide enough to see the possibilities and also the resources to finance this vision. There are many forms of full-time ministry today in the church and all of them have their rightful place in music or drama, in pastoral caring, in youth work or in administration. But there are some dangers. Some desire a full-time Christian ministry in order to escape the greater demands of working in the secular world. There can be a glamour or escapism about Christian ministry and some of us doubt whether all the extension of that ministry today has been truly of the Lord. It is possible to become over-professionalised in our ministry and to lose much in the process. It is equally possible to discourage the amateur or the average church member from participation by having too large a staff or too many people in full-time Christian work. We are called to a wise stewardship, and we need to look at the use of money in payment of salaries to Christian workers alongside the many other needs which challenge our giving.

Ministry is meant to be exercised by every Christian within the local church. The whole concept of spiritual gifts is that they are given for the common good, and Paul expands this idea to suggest that churches should share their resources with one another. That lies behind the very moving chapters 8 and 9 in 2 Corinthians about giving and mutual help. It is not only to do with money, but very much applies to resources of man power. There

117

are areas where churches have too much full-time leadership, and that could be shared with other churches. Sometimes churches that are well resourced are not willing to share and sometimes churches in more deprived areas find it difficult to accept the offers of help from elsewhere. This also applies on a world scale and, thought through, such sharing could have some surprising results. All of us who have travelled around the world in ministry know that this could well be a very beneficial two-way traffic. In our western countries we still have much to offer, but we equally need to be ready to receive and there are younger churches with many gifts to share with us.

We need to recognise that in full-time ministry there are dangers both of over-professionalism and over-specialisation. A minister should be efficient, and he does need to be trained. Equally, the Lord does give different gifts and no man is meant to be skilful in everything. But there is a very real place for the amateur, and most full-time ministry will involve some kind of jack-of-all-trades mentality. It is not true that only the specialist can be effective in his particular job. I believe sincerely that in most pastoral work any full-time ministry needs to be fairly versatile if it is to be effective. Bible colleges and theological colleges need to be alerted to the fact that they are not training specialists but are training all-round men and women, and moreover that they are training them for the real world of today and not for some idealistic church concept that may one day mature. I recollect speaking with a vicar who sadly assured me that his assistant had come from a college where they were very busy preparing men for the twenty-first century, and he was desperately longing for somebody who knew how to cope with the realities of the twentieth, since his congregation had only just moved into that century!

If the full-time minister is something of a one-man band, then it is interesting to find analogies for his position. Perhaps he is like the conductor of an orchestra, who has a very difficult task which is in some ways more demanding than that of a solo intrumentalist. Although I am not a regular devotee of symphony concerts, I recently attended a concert in which the violinist played the solo instrument and was also the conductor. I marvelled at his expertise. In some ways a minister is in that kind of situation. Or perhaps he is not unlike a football player manager, called upon to lead the team, not from the touchline but whilst taking active part himself. Certainly this analogy gets across the point that whether the manager likes it or not 'the buck stops here'. It is part of the heightened tension of Christian work that, although we rejoice in an all-member ministry, there is a very real sense in which we expect the buck to stop in the hands of the full-time minister. It is part of the challenge of leadership to be willing to accept this responsibility and yet with it a willingness to take risks for the sake of the success of the enterprise. If that is true of a leader in the secular world, how much more ought it to be true for those who believe in the Spirit and have every confidence that the cause in which we have invested our lives is the most worthwhile and urgent in the world.

The full-time Christian worker is also a focal point of pastoral care. That care will be shared by many people, but ultimately people relate infinitely better to a person than to a group or a committee. In days gone by the ordained minister in the locality was often known as the 'parson' and I have often wondered whether this was a reference to the fact that he was *the* person in that area to whom people related! Something of that attitude must still remain, and in order for it to work the Christian leader must be seen as a man or woman to be trusted. I have always found it very challenging that in Paul's pastoral epistles he makes it abundantly clear that a man called to leadership within the church should rule his own house well. Domestic arrangements are somewhat different today, but the principle still applies. It ought to be seen that the Christian minister has that ability and therefore can be trusted to be the father of the church family.

In this plea for the value of full-time ministry even today, when the whole church is involved, there is nowhere where it is more urgent than in the preaching ministry. This does not mean to say that the pulpit should always be in the hands or under the feet of one particular man. Certainly it does not assume that the person ordained is necessarily the one with the greatest gifts of preaching. But I believe that congregations benefit most from a consistency of ministry, and that is much more effective when exercised by a limited group of people. Naturally an occasional different voice from the pulpit can be refreshing. Some would argue that in the Keswick Convention two speakers at the main meeting help to give an overall balance to the message, but many would disagree and prefer to have just one message at each Convention meeting. I find it very significant that year after year people comment on the value of the Bible readings at the Keswick Convention, because one man with plenty of time is able to expound a whole tract of Scripture.

There are endless possibilities in this area but I believe that we need to be careful that there should be a preaching ministry from those to whom the gift has been given, who have been commissioned by the church and who have time to give to careful preparation and consistent exposition. Too easily we have assumed that any sincere

Christian can be effective in proclamation. In the Anglican church there has been a strange, topsy-turvy rule that a person needs to have special authorisation to help with Communion, but anyone may have the privilege of appearing in the pulpit with the message, Even in my curacy days I can remember feeling somewhat distressed that I as the ordained minister at a particular time of crisis in the parish was dashing around taking Communion while it was left to lay people to do the preaching. Somehow we seem to have got our priorities utterly upside down.

To stress the importance of the teaching ministry is also to challenge all who believe that they have been called to it or who may be seriously considering the possibility to be ready and willing to be always under the authority of the word of God and in the terms of the prophet, to be ready to tremble at God's word. Such a ministry not only calls for full-time commitment; it also calls for a humble dedication to the task.

This plea for the leader to be the leader must be heard alongside the challenge to a church family to recognise its responsibility towards its minister or full-time leader. There is a great danger of isolation for him and a strange inbuilt expectancy in the church that the minister will somehow ride above depression or disappointment or failure. There is always a significant two-way traffic in ministry. Preaching involves listener as well as speaker in a marvellous harmony. Also pastoral care can never be an isolated experience. It has been for me a painful but liberating experience to share pastoral care with others. In unburdening my own heart in a healthy way I have discovered a deeper love in response from those who share ministry in the church. The pastor needs to be pastored. This is even more important for Christians engaged in itinerant ministry or those working in frontier situations where the loneliness can be extreme. Somewhere, either within the local church family or on a wider front, these people need to be aware that there is a group who are supporting them.

I have been involved in many services of commissioning where the whole congregation expressed its involvement through the laying on of hands by one or two of us in the leadership of the church. Occasionally people have commented about the almost physical sensation of the presence and power of the Lord at such a service, but I have been somewhat sceptical. Indeed, I remain rather fearful of imagining that we can assess the reality of the Spirit by some sort of physical electric shock down our spine! But I must confess that my wife and I were humbled at a service of commissioning in our own church when we were sent out on a special overseas ministry. On that occasion I did sense a semi-physical reaction to the prayerful laying on of hands, and somehow that gave us a reassurance through the coming days of demanding ministry that the congregation was praying for us.

Full-time ministry has many facets, and this chapter has dwelt rather more on the demands of the ordained ministry and the preaching ministry. But in these days there is no greater position of importance than that of youth leadership. In the modern setting, with the challenge of completely unchurched youth and the vital urgency of the need to reach them, it has become a necessity to have more trained people to cope with the situation. Without such leadership and training the church understandably sees any outreach among young people as being quite impossible with the resources of the local church, in terms of manpower, buildings and money. The full-time youth leader will be wise if he spends much of his time in training others to do the actual work in the

122

youth club or its equivalent. A full-time leader will have more time for planning and vision, when normally the demands of just keeping the youth work going is more than the part-time leader can possibly do. It would be living in a fool's paradise to imagine that most local churches could afford the luxury of such a full-time youth leader, but it may well be that churches could join together in appointing someone who could oversee the youth and children's work in a particular area of a city.

Another area where full-time work is needed is the administration of the Christian community. It has been my experience all too often that great ideas never get beyond the drawing board because there is no-one with time or expertise enough to carry them out. These days there are many men and women retiring early with skills of administration and secretarial gifts. We should be able to utilise such resources in the work of the church and thus free those of us who are called to the ministry of preaching the word to do that job effectively. I believe that there was great wisdom in Moses' father-in-law urging the great leader to delegate authority in this area, and in the early church the appointment of the deacons was in the same category.

We need to be careful lest administration takes over the church. We need to be efficient if we are to function effectively in our modern world but we are not primarily a business organisation, and the end product is not efficiency but the winning of souls to Christ. It is all too easy to imagine that once we have organised we have accomplished something. Organisation is just the basis on which we can build through prayer, witness and service.

Similar things could be said about music, so important in the joy of worship. It will be rare for a church or a group to need someone full-time to energise this particular part of church life, but there are those with gifts who need to be freed full-time to help in the wider church in this sphere. Certainly, we cannot afford to allow the music just to happen, but a full-time music worker could sometimes tempt a church to get things out of perspective, as ultimately there is much more to worship than the quality of music.

I believe we need to capture the idea that God has given special gifts to people that should be utilised, since they are gifts of the Spirit. That may mean some people being freed from other work in order to concentrate on this part of the church's ministry.

It would be manifestly unfair within the confines of this chapter to deal with the thorny subject of the ministry of women. Sadly it is now difficult to discuss this without being immediately classified. I have aften agonised when votes on the subject have come before synods of which I have been a member. My instincts are to want to vote for the ordination of women within the Church of England, since there are so many women with gifts which seem to be in that direction, and in all honesty I can conceive of many women doing a far better job as minister of a parish than many men already engaged in that task. But there is always the real problem for an evangelical who believes in the authority of Scripture that it is almost impossible to accept the full ordination of women without apparent disregard of some of the teaching of Scripture. When all allowance is made for differences of culture and we accept that too much must not be built on one or two of Paul's verses in the epistles, the theme of masculine headship does remain as a conisistent Scripture theme right from the book of Genesis (Gen. 3:16; 1 Cor. 11:3; 1 Tim. 2:11).

I personally have no problems about a woman preaching, nor about a woman celebrating Holy Communion. I am certainly not inclined to vote against the ordination of women because of dread of what the Roman Catholic Church would say. That kind of fear leads to no progress at all. But I still hold on to my conviction that Scripture precludes me from voting for the full ordination of women if it means the headship of a local church or of a staff working within that local church. Happily I know that many women would utterly concur with my views. My conscience is clear of all sexism, however subconscious, on this point.

But I will immediately add that I have been learning over the years of the essential value of a woman on the team of leadership in any church in bringing not only particular pastoral gifts but also that indefinable feminine quality and insight. Naturally, I also strongly believe that the wife of a minister or church leader working with the husband is part of that ministry in any case. Increasingly in my own church we have had gatherings of husbands and wives on the staff team when discussing some of the larger issues within church life. There is no other ministry which is so obviously shared and I have often sadly noticed that much effective ministry has been neutralised because husband and wife have not been united in it. Too often it has led to tension in the home and children who have turned away from the church and even from the Lord because of the bad impression gained from a divided home. However, I am equally delighted to testify within my wider ministry that I am always coming across children of ministers and missionaries who are now very much involved in Christian leadership, and seemingly with great maturity, because they have seen ministry in action in a home where there has been unity and happiness in service. I believe that such children, having seen the Lord at work, are eminently suited for Christian leadership and authority in later life.

There is need for strong authority within the church, but with it goes the danger of a new authoritarianism. An echo from Reformation days lingers in my mind: 'new presbyter is but old priest writ large'. Titles will vary from place to place and time to time, but the issue remains the same. A group can be more authoritarian than an individual. Significantly, when the Christian community discovers a new freedom there always comes with it the reverse problem that it will lead into a new authority. We have in recent years through the charismatic movement in particular discovered a new freedom in worship and the exercise of the spiritual gifts. Then inevitably there comes the moment when someone has to decide who has the authority over the prophet, who decides whether or not this is a genuine prophecy and who has authority over the exercise of gifts within the worshipping community. A certain amount of church history always helps on this score, and a study in the fascinating history of the Catholic Apostolic church in the last century is a salutary exercise. What started as a new freedom in the church ended with the renewal of the so-called apostolate of the New Testament pattern and a very strong emphasis on authority.

However much we encourage latent leadership within the Christian community there always will be the need for an ultimate authority. Sometimes this can become very remote from the sphere of action, and it is not only bishops in the Church of England who have this problem. Committees and leadership in many denominations are in danger of the same disease. For those of us who are not in those councils of the church it is intriguing to discover what are the criteria for elevation to positions of importance within a denomination. It has sometimes seemed to be more important to have academic qualifications and to have

126

been involved in church politics than to have been effective within the local church community. What follows then is that there can be a leadership utterly remote from what is really happening within church life, and that is a very dangerous state of affairs.

A study of leadership in Scripture leads you to realise what marvellous surprises God has. He brings a Saul very reluctantly from the backwoods and he discovers a David looking after the sheep; or he captures one of the leaders of opposition like Saul of Tarsus; or he takes a group of fishermen as his main line of attack. Perhaps we have become too predictable as we have looked for leadership. The secret of success where it happened with those biblical leaders was their relationship to God. They were people after his own heart.

The disciples had a double role. They were called by Jesus 'to be with him and to be sent out'. They were appointed as disciples and apostles. There will always be that rhythm in leadership, as in ordinary Christian living. But the leader must supremely be often with the Lord, and yet must be ready to be sent out. He must be fully in tune with his God and equally in tune with the world and the church of his day. I find no condemnation in Scripture of a right kind of ambition to be the best for God. Indeed all the analogies that Paul uses suggest that he expects Christian leaders to pull out all the stops in their service of the Lord and of their fellow Christians. In so doing every leader is utterly dependent upon the Spirit. But it is equally true that the Spirit chooses to work through human agency in normal circumstances. When we consider the battle in which the church is engaged today we need very urgently inspired leadership, and then we need an army mobilised for battle.

9

A Growing Church

—————————— ✍ ——————————

Church growth preoccupies many Christians these days. It is a happy change from the day when we talked pessimistically about the decline of the church. Clearly, high on the agenda of every church must be the prospect of growth. Two of Paul's lovely pictures of the church link at this point. At the end of Ephesians chapter 2 he speaks of the church as a building, a holy temple, growing together with Christ as the cornerstone. Then his picture of the church as a body in Ephesians 4:15-16 also includes this note of growth, and again it must be a growing together. Today we are inspired to expect growth. The danger is that we talk about it and imagine blissfully that it is happening. The statistics give us a little encouragement, but not much more. There are some signs of church attendances growing, and certainly some of us have experienced considerable growth in local churches which we know. I believe it is true to say that the evangelical cause is growing throughout Britain and certainly the concern for evangelism has been growing. It is almost impossible to find criteria which are universally consistent. Certainly, if proliferation of activities and conferences are a sure sign, then the evangelical cause is

128

on the up. But if we are to judge by the impact on society, then I doubt whether we can be quite so optimistic.

The great credal statement of the church that it is 'one, holy, catholic and apostolic' needs to be more closely defined. 'One' does not necessarily mean the onward march of the ecumenical movement; 'holy' certainly does not mean the ghetto mentality which often characterises Christian people; 'catholic' is certainly much wider than Roman Catholic and 'apostolic' has very little to do with the old-fashioned doctrine of the apostolic succession or the insistence of some churches today that the apostolate of the New Testament should be reinstated. A church is only truly catholic if it is following the pattern of the New Testament, where Christians are seen to be 'all one in Christ Jesus', and it is only apostolic if it remains true to the apostles' doctrine enshrined in the New Testament and faithful to the apostolic commission to go out and make disciples of all nations.

In all this the evangelical has been guilty in the past of over-emphasising the individual's response to the gospel and forgetting the corporate element. I have lived through years when the rediscovery of the church has happened, and this has been a great bonus. We have noticed in the New Testament the picture of the church as a whole as the temple of the Holy Spirit. We have responded to the challenge of the Acts of the Apostles, where the whole church bore testimony to the resurrection of Jesus (Acts 4:33). The very life of the church demonstrating the possibility of reconciliation and mutual love has been part of the gospel itself. There can be no doubt that Satan has made his attack upon that spirit of unity, knowing that a divided church is in itself a denial of the gospel. The togetherness of the church must be safeguarded at all costs.

But Satan has another weapon. He loves unbalanced Christians and now is in the business of encouraging people to be so involved in the group and dependent upon it that they miss out on the personal relationship with our Lord. We need to learn to be on our own with God, to develop the good habit of a time of quiet with him. When I became a Christian it was absolutely the norm to tell every young convert that there must be a quiet time and sometimes it became legalistic, causing unnecessary guilt feelings when failure happened. But it was very wise advice, and we are now reaping the whirlwind of having neglected this element of the Christian life. Jesus was very clear on the sermon on the mount that we need to be on our own in prayer and communion with the Lord. Group Bible study is helpful but it is no substitute for personal Bible study. Nor is a selection of devotional thoughts a substitute for deep study. My own strong testimony is that searching the Scripture in depth has brought me closer to the Lord and brought about whatever growth in holiness there has been in my years of pilgrimage. I have also discovered that the devil loves to demolish this individual relationship. I need to be disciplined to hide the word of God in my heart, ready for the hour of testing and to keep very short daily accounts with him.

In the spiritual battle Christian fellowship is a vital ingredient. But just as important is the ability to stand on my own feet in the battle. Paul in Galatians chapter 6 encourages us to bear one another's burdens, but he then goes on to point out that we must carry our own load. Nobody else can take the responsibility for my own spiritual well-being. I stand or fall in that sense on my own two feet. It is interesting that in 1 Thessalonians 4:12 Paul actually tells Christians that they should be 'dependent upon nobody'. There are times when fellowship will not be available. There will be moments of personal testing when not even our closest Christian friend can be of help. We are wise always to heed advice and indeed to seek it. We are equally wise to have our own Christian mind. The apostle Paul listened to the prophets but he did not always follow their advice.

The call to holiness of life is again more than an individual matter. We are called to grow together in the way of holiness, and the expression of holiness will be seen very much in social concern and relationships. Holiness is not just a matter of personal morality. But again, there is no escape from the personal element. We must obey our Lord's command. No corporate experience can by-pass the individual's development. The Spirit indwells the church but he also indwells the individual Christian. We are corporately the temple of the Spirit and we are also individually the temple of the Spirit, therefore called to glorify God in our bodies (1 Cor. 6:19-20). In the language of Jesus the fruit of the Spirit is a very personal experience. In John chapter 15 we are called to abide in Christ, and that is a personal challenge. We only become related to the other branches when we are ourselves closely related to the vine.

As an unrepentant city-dweller I am somewhat hesitant when using horticultural images. I am much happier with the analogies which Paul uses in reference to the body of Christ. In those great chapters, 1 Corinthians 12-14, there is the perfect balance between the individual exercise of the gifts given by the Spirit and yet the awareness of the unity of the body, with each member working for the good and the health of the whole. Paul is at great pains to point out the danger of emphasising the more ecstatic gifts of the Spirit and keeps on underlining the importance of edification. He is equally anxious to ensure that the less

131

obviously gifted people are not made to feel that they have nothing to offer. If only we took the concept of church membership seriously we would always be looking out for the evidence of gifts, which will include those listed in 1 Corinthians chapter 12, but obviously many other gifts as well. Sometimes there will be the natural gifts bestowed by the Creator and sometimes the spiritual gifts which often come with great surprises within the family of God.

Here is a challenge to my own local church which has never been completely accepted. I believe we must encourage a long look at the time, talents and money aspect of Christian stewardship and membership of the church. I believe we need as local fellowships to plan strategically the use of these gifts given by God. Here will be the secret of a growing church ready to meet the demands of today and forming an effective instrument in the hands of the Lord.

In my early Christian experience the gifts were written off as belonging to the apostolic age alone. This was not altogether without some foundation in that many of those gifts were particularly suited to that age. In some ways the gift of prophecy was of less significance once the New Testament was completed, and the church had its final authority. But I believe that the last generation, which thus dismissed these gifts, has in fact contributed to the extremism so often evident in some charismatic circles today. Neglect often has this effect. So a church which has forgotten that supernatural healing happens then creates a church which becomes obsessed with health and healing. A church which neglects teaching the second advent creates a church which becomes unbiblical in its emphasis on this truth. A church which has forgotten the significance of the Jewish people in the economy of God creates a church which becomes obsessed with the geographical Israel. So it is in the matter of spiritual gifts. Many churches today would not receive the rebuke which Paul had to write to the Corinthians. Some of us may need rebuking because we have not taken seriously enough these gifts of the Spirit.

Others amongst us are in the Corinthian position and do need to be warned about excessive enthusiasm for exciting gifts. Paul in 1 Corinthians 12:2-3 suggests that some of the Christians in that church were in danger of being no better than pagans under the influence of their gods. Speaking in tongues was not peculiar to Christianity, nor is it still. The proof that God is at work in this particular gift is that Jesus is honoured and glorified in the life of the person and in the content of what is said. There may be some uncertainties about Paul's directives concerning speaking in tongues in public, but the overall message is very clear. 1 Corinthians 14:18-19 summarises the concern of Paul that Christians in public worship should not appear to have lost control, to be without co-ordination and to appear to the outsider entering church to be utterly mad. I believe that the message needs to be heard again so that we are not obsessed by the ecstatic element in spiritual inspiration.

In playing down one particular gift of the Spirit Paul gives great emphasis to another. It all spills out in the statement of 1 Corinthians 14:1 with its emphasis on prophetic ministry because it produces edification to the whole church, building them up into mature men and women of God. There are two principles that run through these chapters which we need to bear in mind within the community of the church of today. In the first place all these gifts are given for the common good and not primarily for our own personal fulfilment. Secondly love is always the goal. Here is the first fruit of the Spirit. Here is that which every Christian should covet. There is no doubt that Paul's great hymn of praise to love in chapter 13 is far more than an exercise in poetry. It comes as a solemn reminder in these two chapters about gifts that ultimately what counts is the spirit of love. Where that abounds Jesus is being honoured and the Spirit is truly at work.

But there is nothing soft about Christian love. Indeed, it is dynamic and strong, as was the love seen in Jesus. It fits perfectly with the dynamic picture of the church as painted by the apostle in these chapters. When Paul ends 1 Corinthians chapter 14 with a clarion-call for decency and order, he is not talking about the order of blinkered conservatism which will never change. Tragically the church has too often hidden behind this phrase in order to stifle any movement of the Spirit which broke the conventions. When the Spirit is at work there is a dynamism which will break through some of the normal conventions. It is the new wine bursting out of the old wineskins. But that dynamism, if it is to be effective, needs to be channelled, just as the fire of the Spirit needs to be not the bush fire out of control but the controlled fire in which the character of Christ is burned into a man and into society.

Such dynamism not only transforms the local church but makes the fellowship of churches alive in a new way. The gifts are not confined to the local church. As in finance, manpower and expertise, so in the gifts of the Spirit we are challenged to share. I believe that we are meant to see a vision of denominations bringing their particular insights to help each other, that charismatic and non-charismatic under the control of Scripture can strengthen each other. I believe that we can see here a blueprint of how across a city and throughout a country churches can cooperate. Sometimes it means a deliberate

134

policy of moving home to be in the place where my gifts can best be used. All must be under the clear guidance of the Spirit. The great danger is that we stifle his work because of our man-made schemes and our innate fear of change.

Man-made schemes are often the product of man-centred organisations. It would be naive not to note that divisions within the churches are often as much the result of pride and envy as of doctrine and a moving of the Spirit. In all of us there is a battle to fight against these forces. There is no greater tragedy than the oft-repeated one of Christians in rivalry one with another, proselytising in order to feather one's own nest. Everyone rushes to deny this sin but few of us have completely clean hands. Abraham in Genesis chapter 13 had to plead with his nephew Lot that there should be no squabbling in the promised land when pagan nations were watching the people of faith. You can almost hear his tones as he says, 'we are brothers'.

Almost as tragic is the insatiable desire of Christian communities to ape one another. Fashions in worship and in ways of living are often copied, not out of conviction but because we cannot face the possibility of being different. There is the chasing after every novelty which was the hallmark of the Athenians in the day of Paul, but this should never be true of Christians. In the charismatic movement year by year new ideas have appeared, and many of us rush headlong in their direction, whether it be community living or speaking in tongues or prophecy or healing. It may be that the Spirit is saying the same thing at every stage to the same people, but most of us, in all honesty, would have some hesitation to say it was as simple as that. I have been long enough in Christian service to see these swings of the pendulum. Of course, from time to time there is the exact opposite danger of chasing after the old, reformed ideals, such as the idea that exposition must be lengthy to be worth hearing or that illustrations are wrong because they are of the flesh. But may the Lord help us to be true to him, true to his word and courageously true to ourselves.

Fashions come and go very quickly and we need to be clear that we do not lose the ancient paths simply because they are old. I recognise the inherent temptation as a person gets older to look nostalgically to the past. It is a subtle form of personal pride. I recollect as a youngster getting indignant with my father because he told me how much better the cricketers of his generation were. I vowed that it would never happen to me, and now I notice the same thing happening when I discuss a similar subject with my own son. Of that danger we must all be aware, and in realms far more important then cricket. The best is not necessarily in the past, and indeed ultimately it never can be. To live in the past is to fail to live in the present. On the other hand, it is dangerous to cut loose from the past. It is good to read old books as well as new books. It is good to read the sermons of preachers in the past. This is part of belonging to the catholic church which is rooted in the foundation of the apostles and prophets.

Any personal review of church life is bound to be conditioned by individual convictions. I would not for a moment anticipate that every committed Christian leader of today would subscribe to all the views in this book. I shall have failed desperately if that were so, and woe betide the person who is so anxious to please all that he has no convictions left at all. But with that proviso, I do believe that there are important things to be said about the present trends in the church and the way we are moving, and my final chapters will deal with that theme. We need to look at the directions in which the church is going, rejoicing in some exciting new ventures which are still unpredictable and yet being aware of some of the snares which lie in the way. I believe enough in the unity of the church of Jesus to say that it matters that we should be travelling together. We shall be going at different speeds and we shall be going in different ways, but we must see the path before us and dare to travel with him and with one another.

10

A Church at the Crossroads

Speed and travel are the twin main ingredients of our fast-moving society. In such a world the church is in dire danger of being left behind and becoming apparently irrelevant. There is an innate desire in many of us to try to stop the rush of the world's movement and to wish we could get off this fast-moving orb. With such a feeling it is tempting to cherish the church as the great unchangeable. 'Nothing changes here' is a snatch from a great hymn, but it can easily be misunderstood. Anglicans have long ended their psalms by chanting 'as it was in the beginning, is now, and shall be forever'. Deep down we all know that it cannot be but we wish it were. To decide what are unchangables and what must change is one of the most urgent tasks of the church and one of the most controversial.

If it is fatal to refuse to move it is equally fatal to climb on every bandwagon and hail every novelty as the Spirit's leading. Rarely have Christians been so bewildered and confused as now. The challenge to us is to enable a generation which is fearful of change to cope with it and to help a younger generation, often obsessed with the need for immediacy and speed, to understand and appreciate those things that will not change and the true conservationism of the church. In my occasional travels abroad in Christian service I have noted that young people the world over are very much alike and older people are markedly different. Therein lies a hope for the future, but also a challenge.

The church is taking on board much of the technological advance of our day. In my time at one church I have seen the change from a laborious hand duplicator, which in itself was quite a revolution, to a photocopier; from a second-hand typewriter to a brand new computer. Every young minister today is trained in the use of techniques to get across the message and to be more efficient in administration. Those of us from a past age marvel at the possibilities of satellites and a message being literally projected around the world simultaneously. There can be no doubt what this can mean in terms of communication and efficiency. Too often in the past the church has been characterised as amateurish and inevitably second best. This has often been a caricature and there always have been churches giving the best. But there has been reason for the caricature, and now we are able to utilise the techniques to make us as efficient as the rest of the world. But there is a price to be paid, and very often Christians today want efficiency without being ready to give at the level which makes it possible.

Even more important than efficiency, which can all too easily become an idol, is the new ability in communication available to the church today. The Christian world is flooded with films, videos, literature galore and so many translations of the Bible that the preacher becomes bewildered. Never was it more possible for people in the world to hear, to see and to read. The possibility of reaching the world for Christ has now become a realisable objective. Yet somehow with all that possibility there is a feeling of unease.

The efficient minister can very quickly become the impersonal minister. It is all too easy to become removed from the sphere of action, to imagine that to organise something is to accomplish something. Sometimes we are so conscious of administration that we do not find the time to listen to people, to get to know their real problems and therefore to be able to counsel them. It may be a symbol of our day that one of the latest popular activities in church is ministering to one another after worship. Very easily we imagine that some moments in prayer after a service can take the place of long hours of listening, discussing and praying. There is a place for the after-service ministry, but it would be madnesss to imagine that we have discovered a quick way to solve problems. If the modern techniques make contact more possible they also make more demands upon people who should be in touch with real life and be able to give time to real people. May the church be aware of the dangers and may the Spirit keep us human and able in our humanity to communicate as person to person.

In days of instant, packaged food we can be tempted to believe that we can live on a diet of instant, packaged religion. It sounds attractive to be able to have it all so easily and neatly parcelled up for us. But the fruit of the Spirit grows over a period, and constantly in the New Testament we are exhorted to hard work and effort, prayer and service, so that we can obtain the results. We are constantly reminded that if we cannot achieve anything without him, he certainly will not do it without us, because he is concerned about our character. There is no short cut to holiness or to spiritual maturity. Therefore we need in days of modern technology to allow the technology to be our servant and not our master.

One of the common activities of today is blaming the media. On many occasions this can be a get-out clause when we have our backs to the wall. There is much truth in the accusations about the media's desire for excitement and an immediate story, with issues blown up out of all proportion. But the church must learn to use the media and not be used by them. We would be missing God-given opportunities if we did not utilise the openings given to us by the press, radio and television. Apart from anything, it means that we can project the Christian message into areas that are otherwise completely untouched by it: into geographical areas where the church is persecuted and also to different groups of society where there is no contact whatever with the good news of the gospel. It would be possible to write many books demonstrating the powerful effects of the gospel through the media, and that is the unique opportunity of today.

The media do not create the personality cult, but they certainly multiply the danger. Many of us have been sickened by examples of the religious soap opera from across the Atlantic. There is something almost blasphemous about the misuse of the gospel in order to gain money, position and power. The church throughout the world is particularly vulnerable to this kind of approach. We are an age desperately looking for leadership, and a leader with a certain charisma, who is treated with favour by the media can do untold harm. If in the New Testament there is evidence of the danger of personalities being exalted beyond degree by the applause of men, consider how much more dangerous that is today. Without venturing into apocalyptic prophecy, I could easily produce a scenario in which some quite unprincipled man or woman used this religious media platform to project a false gospel that would win millions.

The day of the antichrist is very much on our doorstep, and we need to be aware of the dangers. Some of the more sinster elements in the prophecies of the book of the Revelation seem not too far distant and certainly not far-fetched.

A famous historian commented that 'all power corrupts; absolute power corrupts absolutely'. This is not only true on the stage of political history but can all too often be true on the stage of church history. It has always been a temptation to be put on a pedestal, and often the Christian leader can find pedestals to spare. It is a marvel that a man in the public eye as much as Billy Graham has kept so humble and usable. Nowhere in the remarkable story of that man is the power of prayer more obvious than at this point. But many lesser men have succumbed to money and position. Christians have been led astray by those who have used religion as a cloak for selfish ends. Our world is desperate for leadership, and the church is no exception. The tragedy of a leadership which is often weak and ineffective makes it all the more dangerous for the person with leadership quality. Constantly in Christian history, and we see it often repeated today, there are those who come on to the scene with some new vision and new ideas. It is very important that Christians should learn the art of discrimination and remember the apostle John's command that we should test the spirits. We must not quickly accept every person or movement that claims to be a new revelation from God.

Somewhat less sinister but equally disturbing is the success syndrome which is often preached today. Taking Old Testament promises quite out of context, we are exhorted to expect that the good Christian will always be successful and become wealthy. Even when this is not being criminally exploited, it is a travesty of the truth.

Of course, we are not meant to deify failure, and very often in the past the church has been content to be second-rate and on the losing side. Equally, it is not a sin to be wealthy – just a challenge to know how to use that wealth. But the sign of the Christian faith is not success but the cross. That which the world counts as the greatest failure is the message which the apostle Paul would always preach and by which the church has always conquered. We follow one who was in the world's eyes a failure and rejected. It is ironic that in some streams of the church today we have to present success to demonstrate that the Spirit is at work. There is no evidence in Scripture that God means everyone to be healthy, wealthy and fully employed. We need to expose those who insist that this is the supreme mark of God at work. Some of the greatest saints in history have suffered much, have been rejected by their fellows and have lived in abject poverty.

Since the church is always liable to be infected by the spirit of the age, we are not only under pressure from the ideal of success, but we are also pressurised by a society which exalts the instant and the immediate. Christians become impatient with the gospel which talks of gradual growth in holiness. We want everything at once and assume that there is a package deal which can give us instant holiness. New Testament spirituality takes time, and some of its greatest blessings are reserved for heaven and will never be known on earth. The body will be resurrected and only then will be perfectly whole. It is essential to remember Paul's comment in 2 Corinthians 4:16 that 'though our outer nature is wasting away, our inner nature is being renewed every day'. In his mercy God chooses to heal people on earth, and in answer to prayer and the laying on of hands miracles happen, and we must never cease to expect God to work in these ways.

143

But we have no right to assume that perfect health is our birthright as Christians. Only in heaven will the body be free from pain and from the ravages of time. It is also true that Christian virtues grow and develop gradually and that the process of becoming like our Lord may have its moments of glorious progress, but will also have battles and many occasions of apparent stalemate. We have no promise of quick success in the realm of holiness, which is the greatest concern for every Christian.

It is probably also one of the marks of our day – and the church has caught it – that excitement is the yardstick of success. We are more inclined to exalt the spectacular rather than the solid and dependable. This is not to suggest that we should opt happily for dullness, but the New Testament does call frequently for sobriety, for balance and self-control. It would be hard to imagine that our Lord's pathway to Calvary was exciting. The apostle Paul condemns the Corinthian Christians because they were much more thrilled about the gifts which were exciting than the ones which contributed to edification and maturity. I sometimes believe that I have been given a crusade to convince young people in particular that the balance of the New Testament is indeed thrilling. Those of us who are shut into the biblical balance should never allow those who have apparently more exciting experiences to set the agenda. I believe we have often been guilty of a strange kind of inferiority complex, and wait for exciting movements to produce the latest fad and then seek to respond to it. I believe that we have reached the stage when Christians have had more than enough of the excitement and are waiting desperately for something which truly satisfies. The celebration element in Christianity should not be omitted, but we are certainly not called to be living in one long party atmosphere. Even parties stale after a while. The Christian life is not a game or a performance, but is life worth living.

There is also about our age a disturbing exaltation of the childish. Simplicity is often taken to extremes, and in the Christian church we have become almost fearful of the adult mind and the use of the intellect. The simple chorus has its place in worship, but mindless repetition is a dangerous exercise. Childishness is seen in our moving from one toy to another. There is an insatiable desire for novelties in our world and in our church. The great discovery of today becomes outdated in a week. In the world this tendency is merely a nuisance; in the church it can be quite disastrous.

In some ways this is a form of escapism from the grim realities of the world and the insistent demands of the instant media. We cannot be unaware of the sufferings of humanity. Within minutes they are in all our homes and sometimes the burden of seeking to enter into a suffering world becomes too great. With all the negative comments about the church of today, one of its greatest positives is a new level of caring for a world of need. The world has suddenly become small and on our doorstep. But it is still a minority of Christians who take stewardship seriously, who are ready to share their resources at the kind of level which the New Testatment envisages.

In our own church, when we felt that the Lord was leading us to extend our church buildings, we were very concerned that this should not be at the expense of the starving millions and of a world dying without the knowledge of Christ. Without rationalising our position, we could easily have justified the expenditure on buildings if they were used to reach more people with the message of the gospel, which would challenge them to live lives of dedicated stewardship. But we must always be mindful of the danger of building our barns larger in the Western world and forgetting or shutting our ears to the heart-cry of our suffering brethren. Nor is it a matter only of the Third World. Christians need not be ashamed to be called middle-class, but they must be ashamed if they subscribe too easily to the divisions in our own society which are rapidly making us a nation of two halves, each hardly understanding the other.

It has been my privilege to be brought up within a largely working-class community, sharing its joys and understanding some of its tensions. I am grateful that I have never forgotten these lessons, and I testify that the Lord has given me a deep desire to demonstrate that the class barriers are down in Jesus Christ. My ministry has widened in every kind of way within this country and throughout the world, and with it I have felt a challenge to a principle of action which is vital to my own peace of mind. I have always sought to treat all people, whatever their background, in exactly the same way. In that I have by no means always succeeded, but I am conscious when failure comes. Sometimes the church has been guilty of bowing before the social structures of our day and not daring to speak prophetically against them.

The church of today has a unique opportunity to demonstrate that unity which is ours in Christ and which does transcend national and cultural barriers. It could be one of the greatest demonstrations of the truth of the gospel. In Paul's day this horizontal reconciliation of man with man was a proof of the vertical reconciliation between man and God, and so it must be today. If in the church we cannot proclaim this unity, then our world is indeed lost. I believe we must have a crusade to show to a fearful world that there is a place where men and women can live and love together.

But paradoxically, in a world where there is often a lack of reconciliation, there is also a fanatical desire to copy one another. Our world seems to be losing individuality and becoming stereotyped. If that is true in the world, it is tragically often true in the church. We are so anxious to keep up with the Jones' spiritually. We are in danger of following every fashion. I would urge Christians to seek to be themselves in the service of their Lord. Another aspect of our society which impinges on the church is the deep desire for tolerance, and the suggestion that any intolerance is the greatest of all sins. It is very difficult for people to dare to suggest, for example, that all religions are not working together. Syncretism has always been a danger from Old Testament days, and I have found it necessary to refuse to be involved in joint religious services where Christians, Muslims, Jews, Hindus and Buddhists pretend that they worship the same God. It takes courage to suggest that Jesus is unique, and we dare not let any other share his throne.

A retrospective look at the thirty years of my ministry also encourages me to rejoice that there has been a proliferation of Christian conferences and conventions. No longer does Keswick have the monopoly. No longer is it an accolade of evangelicalism to be involved in the ministry of Keswick, and that is altogether a good thing. It is thrilling to see so many people gathering in groups like Filey/Skegness, Spring Harvest and the various other convention groups to seek the Lord's will, to enjoy fellowship together, to listen to the Spirit and to respond in service. It is equally good that there is a variety of approach, and it would be foolish for the Conventions to seek to ape one another. But I confess that there is a danger of dilution by extension. It is good for Christians to have a variety of choice, but not always are they mature enough to make the choice wisely. As the Chairman of the Keswick Convention Council I must believe that we have something very special to offer. We dare not claim a monopoly of concern about Christian holiness, nor would I suggest that only in the Keswick manner is the word of God expounded effectively. May we be saved from all arrogance.

Nor dare we keep the traditions of Keswick within a mould which has been blessed in the past but which may not be suitable for a younger generation. I recollect a younger friend suggesting to me after his first visit to the Keswick Convention a year or two ago that he would be happy to recommend to his student friends the commodity which Keswick is offering. But he was very unhappy about the packaging and felt that some might not see through the packaging to the treasure within. I believe we at Keswick are challenged to make the old-fashioned message of personal, practical and scriptural holiness alive and exciting for today. I happen to believe that the Christian way is not always meant to be spectacular and miraculous. Signs and wonders may be seen in the very normal and ordinary ministry of the word of God and the Spirit applying it to the human heart. But I do want something that has stood the test of time to be relevant and contemporary.

I have noticed during these decades a proliferation of training sessions and systems. It is possible now to train for every aspect of church life and courses with attractive brochures abound. The church leader and minister is inundated with the latest ideas, and if he were to take notice of every circular which reached his desk, he and his congregation would be at training courses and special weekends all the year round. It is possible to train so effectively that you never have time to do anything. I have often discovered that the most effective Christians are people who have had precious little training. But there is a danger of cynicism, and I accept the fact that we should rejoice that such expertise is available in the life of the church.

I am equally unsure whether the multiplicity of Christian books is altogether a bonus blessing in our day. The Preacher in Ecclesiastes lamented that there was no end of making many books. Christians are often bewildered when they look at the display on the bookshelves. There is a real danger that we feed ourselves on very light books and prefer an exciting experience story to a book of sermons or a commentary or doctrine. Yet again we have to keep the balance. No Christian now need go untaught. I wonder, however, how many do read regularly, and I have been distressed from time to time to discover how few Christians, with all the translations of Scripture available, read them regularly and systematically.

As a servant of the Lord I believe without any doubt that he has called me to the kingdom for such a time as this. I do believe that the church of Jesus is basically stronger than it was when first I began my ministry. With all the reservations and the need to be somewhat sceptical about some of the great claims of today, I am sure that there is every evidence that the Spirit of the Lord is at work. We are handing on a church equipped and ready to meet the enormous challenges of the world bursting upon us. We must look backward and remember our heritage; we must look forward and trust our Saviour. It is no trite saying that the best is yet to be.

11

Perspectives

—————————— 🌿 ——————————

Middle age has many advantages. It is still possible to look backward without a memory too impaired or a tendency to believe that the days that are past were the best. At the same time it is possible still to look forward with eagerness for ministry here as well as the hope of heaven hereafter. There is still the excitement of things new – even of writing this first book, with a mixture of excitement and trepidation. I believe that middle age, however that period of life may be defined, is the crucial battleground in the church. Young people matter enormously and old people must not be neglected, but the church needs a vigorous middle age, with maturity yet with some youthful fire and vision.

From that middle-aged standpoint I can see that there is no doubt that God is very evidently at work today, and often in a way which in youth we had not seen. Nobody can doubt the reality of the Spirit's work and the signs of supernatural activity among us. Inevitable some go overboard, and there are casualties of excess. There are also dangers of forgetting some of the great theological battles which have been won in the past. We do not wish to have to fight them again. This is particularly true of the battle over the authority of Scripture. With all the joy of a new sense of belonging to one another in the family of Christ, there is now the great danger of division along other lines and even among decidedly evangelical Christians.

As I look to the future from my vantage point it is largely with optimism, because we have a God who is always liable to break through in some new way. But the hope is not just vague and a matter of principle. There is enough evidence of God at work in the present to give us that hope. But oddly enough, it is not the more manifest signs of activity that give me that hope, and certainly not the wild innovations of our day. It is the steady consistency of the growth of the church, even through days of testing and days of division. Here is a basis for future hope.

I have always been fascinated by the moments in Scripture when one great man of God hands on the task to another. This is the baton change in the spiritual marathon. Moses hands over to Joshua; Elijah to Elisha; our Lord to his disciples; Paul to Timothy. That last chapter of Paul's second letter to Timothy is a very moving exposition of an older man looking back and looking forward. Paul sees things differently as he seeks to see them through the eyes of young Timothy. He is more concerned that the work should continue than he is for his own reputation. That chapter has many solemn words to say to some older Christian leaders who cannot hand over and who find it hard to believe that God can work through different personalities and in different ways, but with the same goal in mind.

Paul can look back with a clear conscience as he looks at his ministry. There is no arrogance in Paul's sense of achievement. He never forgets that he is the chief of sinners, and he is very aware of his failures. But he can speak of the total thrust of his life in terms of the fight finished, the race run and the faith loyally kept. In the context of that chapter there is a very marked contrast with Demas in verse 10, who started well but gave up the race because of his 'love for this present world'. It may have been materialism that wooed Demas away or a fear of being too committed. It could be costly to follow a man like Paul. There is always the danger of Christians giving up the race because the going is too hard.

Paul's testimony should be a great encouragement, and certainly the future of the kingdom will depend upon that kind of faithfulness. Paul was anxious to hand on the faith unimpaired to the next generation. That kind of apostolic succession is of the first importance today. We belong to a good heritage, and we must never forget the glories of the past. But those who have known these glories should want to see yet greater things in the future.

Because he looks back with a clear conscience, Paul can look forward with a calm confidence, and that is seen in 2 Timothy 4:6-8, with its assurance of an eternal reward and death as mere departure from this world. The Greek word has the note of a boat slipping out to sea, or a tent being moved, or a riddle being answered or a knot being untied. It is so vital to live our Christian life in the light of that death. There should always be a heightened urgency, since that day could come at any time and yet also an increased desire to share a hope which so many in our day cannot possibly have. Equally, there is nothing sub-Christian in looking on to the day of reward, with the proviso that we accept it as not our desert but as God's grace. There may have been a time when heaven was too much in people's minds. We certainly live now in a day when it is almost forgotten.

The historic perspective of Paul's last words has a

parallel in our day. It is very easy for those of us who boldly fly the evangelical flag today to forget that a generation or two ago there was a very obvious stigma about being known as an evangelical and daring to believe in the gospel. It has not altogether gone, but we do live in very different days and we have a debt to those who held the gospel high when it meant subtle persecution and rejection, often by their fellow churchmen. Different denominations have had different experiences. Wearing my Anglican hat, I know only too well that many men in a generation before mine suffered much because they stood true, and I believe we must honour them constantly. In a different way the same perspective is seen in the world church, with men who often laboured hard with few evident results in their day, so that we today might reap the benefit. My visits abroad and insights into the growth of the Christian church in places like Nigeria, India and Japan have taught me vital lessons. As I have heard about missionaries or local Christians who suffered much, as I have stood in a graveyard with headstones to children who died not too many years ago because their parents went into areas of disease and lack of hygiene – at such moments I realise how great a debt the church of today owes to the sacrifice of men and women of a bygone age. That spirit must still be with us, even if we live in very different days and the tests are not quite so obvious.

As the apostle Paul looked to the future in his day, he knew how much depended upon the younger generation taking up the challenge. So he brings his exhortation to Timothy, and that exhortation begins with a challenge to 'preach the word' (2 Tim. 4:2). The command suggests the idea of a very definite commitment. It will be an ongoing work, but every now and again the Christian minister must renew his commitment to make this proclamation the priority of his life. I rate that as one of the greatest needs for today. There can be no substitute for dynamic, convincing proclamation of the truth. Many of the aids towards preaching can easily become our masters and the resurgence of a concern for worship can drive out preaching. Satan is very subtle. Often his attacks would go along the line of our spirituality and our service. He will encourage ministers to be obsessed with secondary issues and miss out the primaries.

Then Paul becomes more specific with his concern for 'sound teaching' (verse 3). In his day there was a great deal of teaching which was moving away from the basic truths of the gospel in order to be popular, in order to suit the likings of the hearers. We see that temptation constantly in the Bible. It was there in the days of Jeremiah, who battled with the false prophets. A meditation in Jeremiah chapter 23 could be very salutary for us today. The true preacher will proclaim the message without fear or favour. he will certainly not allow the congregation to dictate in the sense of anaesthetising his message so that no one will feel hurt or upset. Nor will the preacher who follows in the footsteps of Paul ever fall into the temptation of making his message intellectually respectable to those who stand critically outside the gospel. Paul is ready to be thought a fool, and so must we. It is vital to be intellectually honest; it is disastrous to seek to be intellectually respectable. These verses remind Timothy that it is very easy to 'wander into myths' (verse 4). The verb speaks of a gradual move from the centrality of scripture into man-made schemes and man-pleasing teaching. Paul remembers that he had been opposed by a formidable opponent in Alexander the coppersmith (verse 13). He has had many successors, and we must dare to stand up to those who deny the truth of the gospel. The apostolic message can be diluted by liberalism or by an experience-centred message. Jeremiah condemns those who are always referring to their visions and dreams. Let us be those who keep true to Scripture at any cost.

But Paul is not primarily concerned about orthodoxy for its own sake. Sound teaching speaks of wholesome or healthy teaching, and his concern is to build up the people of God. Therefore the message must not only be scripturally true but relevant and driven home with true prophetic conviction. Three verbs underline this sense of urgency: 'convince, rebuke and exhort' (verse 2). That may only be done by a person who is seen to care for his people. There must be a pastoral relationship to give the preacher the right to speak in this kind of way. It will mean an urgency, a readiness to speak 'in season and out of season', and a patient availability. 'A word fitly spoken is like apples of gold in a setting of silver' (Prov. 25:11). Some proclamation is done from a safe distance, and with all its accuracy is ineffective. The true man or woman of God will relate the unchanging truths of the word of God to the rapidly changing world of today and by the Spirit of God make it often uncomfortably relevant.

The overall theme of this book is summed up in the qualities commended in 2 Timothy 4:5. There is a call to be steady, sober or dependable. How subtle is the temptation to opt for the exciting rather than the solid and lasting. There is also a call to endure suffering. Serving the Jesus of the New Testament, we must be ready for that element at the very centre of our Christian living. Beware of an easy success story. Our Lord did not aim to be a successful man, but to be a suffering servant, and that is our call. In an age which is obsessed with health, we have almost forgotten the value of a suffering ministry. There needs to be in the truest sense of the word a new martyr spirit and a readiness to be hardy and tough in the Lord's service. We see all around us fanaticism for unworthy or evil causes. Christians are not meant to be fanatics but we are certainly meant to demonstrate that the gospel of Jesus is worth suffering, worth hard work and if necessary worth life itself.

The third quality asked of Timothy is that he should do the work of an evangelist (verse 5). Some may have a particular calling, a gift for this ministry. All that we know of timid Timothy suggests that he was not the evangelist indentikit type. But his ministry would not be fulfilled without this element. It is easy to lose sight of the fate of the lost and the need to win them to Christ. It is tempting to be fully occupied with the care and problems of fellow Christians. But at the heart of all church life must be the priority of evangelism. Without that all our pastoral care will become stale. A church which is not constantly involved in evangelism and receiving new Christians will never have the life of the New Testament about it.

At the end of 2 Timothy 4:5 Timothy is called to fulfil his ministry. It is a call to have a fully-rounded ministry. The Bible is full of the note of being filled. We are exhorted to be filled with the Spirit; we are offered the prospect of being full of joy, and there is a lovely phrase in the Old Testament where some of the saints are said to have died 'full of years'. It does not just speak of old age. It speaks of people whose lives have gone full circle. You can live long and uselessly. You can live briefly and effectively. God means us to be truly fulfilled in his service.

All of this must be seen in the solemn words in 2 Timothy 4:1, a reminder that we do all our Christian service in the light of a God who searches the heart and of a Jesus who will one day return in judgement. That drives us out with an urgent eagerness, since we never know the day when our Lord will return. Living as we do in world crisis days, it is not hard to imagine the final denouement being around the corner. But equally the Christian is called to serve in the light of the Lord's final victory. Such a conviction will make us infinitely less concerned about judgements by our fellow men and even about our own self-judgement. So Paul can speak in 1 Corinthians 4:3-5. To be saved from the tyranny of public opinion and the tyranny of my own view of myself is a great liberation. To live in the awareness of God's searching gaze and the Lord's certain return is the way to find that liberation. It means being motivated by the fear of the Lord in the deepest sense.

I recollect reading the story of one of the saints of a Scottish revival of a century ago as he spoke to his great friend, the wonderful Scottish preacher Murray McCheyne, about the urgency of the hour in a very simple phrase: 'Brother, we must hurry'. That phrase has always remained with me. We do not know the day of our Lord's return. We do not know how much more service he will allow us to have. We may not easily assess the health or vitality of the church of today. We may not be sure whether we should be gloriously optimistic or soberly realistic. But we are called to be faithful in the hour he has given us for service. We owe it to our generation not to be found wanting in loving service and effective evangelism. In the deepest theological sense the time is short. Let us keep moving and keep the church on the move for the sake of Jesus and the gospel.

Other Marshall Pickering Paperbacks

THE KINGDOM FACTOR

Roger Mitchell

We are living in extraordinary days. The rains of revival are on the way. The cloud is already bigger than a man's hand. All over the world is a resurgence of living Christianity. The coming in of the Kingdom of God in our generation is a real possibility. Whether or not this movement of God's spirit will finally bring the return of Jesus and the universal Kingdom of God will depend on the size of our vision of Jesus, the depth of our fellowship together in the Holy Spirit and the success of our evangelism. This can be the generation.

This is the thrust of evangelist Roger Mitchell's powerful book challenging Christians to bring in the Kingdom of God and to proclaim to a world desperately seeking answers that it is not some vague future hope, but a solid present.

WHEN YOU PRAY

Reginald East

Spiritual renewal has awakened in many Christians a deeper longing to know God more intimately. Prayer is the place where we personally meet God, yet it is often treated simply as the means for making requests for our needs, and offering our stilted, dutiful thanks. In this practical guide to prayer, Reginald East shows how we can establish a prayer relationship with God which is both spiritually and emotionally satisfying. Through understanding God and ourselves better, prayer can truly become an encounter with God, where we relax into Him, enjoy Him, listen as well as talk to Him and adventure into discovering His heart of love.

MY FAITH

Compiler: Mary Elizabeth Callen

Well-known Christians invite us in through their private doors to reveal fascinating glimpses of their most personal thoughts and deepest convictions about their faith.

The late Laura Ashley and her husband frequently turned to the Bible for advice on her growing business. Botanist David Bellamy knows who to thank for all he enjoys in life. At 102, Catherine Bramwell-Booth still lives to spread the message of Christ. Lord (Len) Murray found God in the poverty of London's East End. The presence of Christ transformed the agony of torture into 'a privilege' for Dr Sheila Cassidy. For Anne Watson, God became more real and more mysterious during her husband David's illness and death.

Their moments of peace, doubt, anger and pure joy are common to us all, yet their experiences confirm the uniqueness of God's love for each individual.

FORGIVE AND RESTORE

Don Baker

When a member of God's family, in this case a loved pastor, goes seriously off the rails in his personal life, the question looms large, 'What should the Church do about it?' 'Is it a matter for the church leadership only?' Should the wayward member be asked to leave or just relieved of responsibility? What should the congregation be told?

This book is a remarkable account of how one church dealt with such a highly charged and emotional crisis. It records in honest detail the ebb and flow of hope and despair, uncertainty and humanity, and relying throughout on biblical principles, it picks its way through a tangled mess to find a place of healing and restoration again.

If you wish to receive *regular information* about *new books*, please send your name and address to:

London Bible Warehouse
PO Box 123
Basingstoke
Hants RG23 7NL

Name...

Address ....

....

....

....

I am especially interested in:
☐ Biographies
☐ Fiction
☐ Christian living
☐ Issue related books
☐ Academic books
☐ Bible study aids
☐ Children's books
☐ Music
☐ Other subjects